The Ultimate Canadian Cookbook

111 Dishes From Canada To Cook Right Now

Slavka Bodic

Copyright @2021

All rights reserved. No part of this book may be reproduced in any form without writing permission in writing from the author. Reviewers may quote brief passages in reviews.

No part of this publication may be reproduced or transmitted in any form or by any means, mechanical or electronic, including photocopying or recording, or by any information storage and retrieval system, or transmitted by email without permission in writing from the publisher. While all attempts have been made to verify the information provided in this publication, neither the author nor the publisher assumes any responsibility for errors, omissions or contrary interpretations of the subject matter herein.

This book is for entertainment purposes only. The views expressed are those of the author alone and should not be taken as expert instruction or command. The reader is responsible for his or her actions. Adherence to all applicable laws and regulations, including international, federal, state and local governing professional licensing, business practices, advertising, and all other aspects of doing business in US, Canada or any other jurisdiction is the sole responsibility of the purchaser or reader.

Neither the author nor the publisher assumes any responsibility or liability whatsoever on the behalf of the purchaser or reader of these materials. Any perceived slight of any individual or organization is purely unintentional. Similarity with already published recipes is possible.

Imprint: Independently published

Please sign up for free Balkan and Mediterranean recipes:
www.balkanfood.org

Introduction

Do you want to celebrate the authentic Canadian flavors by cooking some delicious and savory meals at home? Then you have found the right fit for you! This cookbook will introduce you to some of the most popular Canadian recipes and meals that you'll definitely love, especially if you're a food lover. Whether you have been to Canada or not, you can recreate its traditional cuisine at home with the help of this comprehensive cookbook. Canada is popular for its unique culture, languages, and food. As a result, this cookbook is a simple way to come close to the flavorsome cuisine of this North American region.

The Ultimate Canadian Cookbook will showcase Canadian cuisine and its culinary culture in a way that you may have never tried before. It brings you a variety of Canadian recipes in one place. The cookbook is perfect for all those who always wanted to cook Canadian food on their own, without the help of a native Canadian. Based on this Canadian cuisine cookbook, you can create a complete Canadian menu, or you can try all the Canadian recipes on different occasions as well. In this cookbook, you'll find popular Canadian meals and ones that you might not have heard of yet.

In these recipes, you'll discover some of the most commonly used Canadian ingredients like veggies and meat. Not only that, but you'll also learn how to make such ingredients and use them in different meals. The Canadian cuisine has been comprised of various dishes of the

Canadian people and has been widely spread across the globe. There's a clear difference between taste and flavor in the food of various regions of Canada due to the differences in culture and geological locations. And in this cookbook, you'll obtain all the recipes from different parts of Canada.

Here's what you'll gain in this cookbook:
- Insights about Canada and Canadian cuisine
- Canadian breakfast recipes
- Snacks and appetizers
- Salads and side meals
- Canadian soups
- Main dishes
- Canadian desserts and drinks

Let's try all these Canadian Recipes and recreate a complete menu to celebrate the amazing Canadian flavors and tantalizing aromas.

Table of Contents

INTRODUCTION 3
WHY CANADIAN CUISINE? 9
CANADA 11
BREAKFAST 13
    Pumpkin and Oat Pancakes 14
    Buttermilk Pancakes 15
    Pumpkin Bread 16
    Canadian Fried Dough 18
    Cheddar-Ham Oven Omelet 20
    Cheddar Loaves 21
    Sonrisa's Butter Tart Squares 22
    Canadian Tea Biscuits 24
    Browned Butter Banana Bread 25
    Easter Hot Cross Buns 26
    Mushroom Bouchees 28
    Slow Cooker Western Omelets Brunch Bake 29
    Partridgeberry Banana Pancakes 31
    Breakfast Poutine 33
    Coconut and Flaxseed Toast 35
    Montreal Bagels 36

APPETIZERS 37
    Canadian Bacon Cheese Straws 38
    Creamy Caramel Dip 40
    Cheddar Pan Rolls 41
    Air-Fryer Crispy Sriracha Spring Rolls 43
    Authentic Canadian Poutine 45
    Cheese Spread 47
    Mushroom and Bannock Bites 48
    Classic Canadian Butter Tarts 50
    Pea Meal Bacon 52
    Grilled Oysters 53
    Cinnamon-Sugar Snowshoes 54
    Maple-Fennel Bacon 56

SALADS 57

    Fennel Salad with Citrus Dressing 58
    Canadian Pub Salad 59
    Canadian Caesar Salad 60
    Tomato and Orzo Summer Salad 61
    Chicken Waldorf Wedge Salad 62
    Macaroni Salad 63
    Avocado and Grilled Corn Salad 64
    Grilled Peach and Tomato Salad 65
    Fennel and Radicchio Salad 67
    Canadian Cobb Salad 68

SOUPS 70

    Canadian Cheese Soup 71
    Cream of Celery Soup with Seared Scallops 73
    Cream of Parsnip Soup with Broccoli and Cranberries 75
    Ontario Butternut Squash Soup 77
    Chicken Squash Soup 78
    Alberta Soup 79
    Newfoundland Dumpling Soup 80
    Friend's Bean Soup 82
    Hearty Tuscan Soup 83
    Acorn Squash Soup with Warm Spices 84
    Cilantro-Lime Chicken Soup 86
    Turkey and White-Bean Soup 88
    Classic Soup with Chicken and Shrimp 89
    Canadian Yellow Split Pea Soup with Ham 90
    Mushroom Soup 91
    Beefy Barley Soup 93
    Tomato Soup with Grilled Cheese Croutons 94
    Canadian Vegetable Soup 96
    Mushroom, Barley and Bacon Soup 98

MAIN DISHES 99

    Montreal Smoked Meat 100
    Glazed Cornish Hens with Pecan-Rice Stuffing 102
    Duo Tater Bake 104
    Sticky Honey Chicken Wings 106
    Cranberry Maple Chicken 107
    Caribou Canadian Stew 108

Canadian Beef Stew	110
Hodge Podge	112
Chunky Creamy Chicken Stew	113
Cauliflower Stew	114
Turkey Tetrazzini	115
Sweet Potato Stuffing	117
Scalloped Potatoes	118
Pastry-Topped Turkey Casserole	119
Baked Chicken Schnitzel	121
Greek Lemon Chicken and Potato Bake	122
Danielle's Seafood Chowder	123
Salmon and Potato Pie	125
Best Fried Walleye	126
Sautéed Fiddleheads	127
Real Poutine	128
Holiday Tourtiere	129
Oven-Fried Potatoes	**131**
Crispy Ginger Beef	132
Canadian Tourtiere	134
Canadian Pork Loin Chops	136
Christmas Brunch Casserole	138
DESSERTS	**140**
Filled Strawberries	141
Canadian Cinnamon Rolls	142
Caramel Fudge Cheesecake	144
Peanut Butter Graham Bars	145
Old-Fashioned Buttermilk Biscuits	146
Cranberry Butter Crunch Bark	147
Chocolate Peanut Butter Candy	148
Mint Angel Cake	149
Gramma's Date Squares	150
Canadian Squares	151
West Coast Trail Cookies	153
Vancouver Island Cookies	155
Classic Butter Tarts	157
Duchess Doughnut	159
Apple Dutch Baby	161
PB&J Bites	162
Butterscotch Fudge	163
Cherry Nanaimo Bars	164

Maple Meringues 166
　　　Nanaimo Bars 167
　　　Rhubarb Crumble Ice Cream 169
　　　Chocolate-Covered Cheesecake Squares 170

DRINKS **172**
　　　Canadian Cocktail 173
　　　Classic Caesar 174
　　　Canadian Maple Old-Fashioned 175
　　　Canadian Punch 176
　　　Canadian Whiskey Sour 177

ONE LAST THING **186**

Why Canadian Cuisine?

Canadian cuisine varies from region to region as the country has a diverse culinary culture and population. The four cuisines that Canada received to early migrations of people from other parts of the world brought food of Scottish, First Nations, English, and French origins. Traditional Canadian cuisine is deeply influenced by British cuisine.

The 16th-century French cuisine then influenced the traditional Canadian cuisines when the New French colonials came to this place. Now the French-Canadian cuisine is further divided into Québécois cuisine and Acadian cuisine.

People from Central, Eastern, and Southern Europe brought their culinary culture to Canada along with them during the 19th and 20th centuries. Regional Canadian cuisines were further affected by Caribbean, East Asian, and South Asian cuisines. Due to all these influences, it's hard to pinpoint any single dish or any particular cooking style as being truly Canadian. It has been said that "Canada has a cuisine of cuisines, not a stew pot but a smorgasbord."

In fact, numerous recipes are termed as Canadian specialties. Some of the popular meals from this North American region include the following:

- Best Fried Walleye
- Pea meal bacon
- Nanaimo bars
- Oven-Fried Potatoes
- Southwest Shepherd's Pie with Mashed Cauliflower
- Canadian Tourtiere
- Christmas Brunch Casserole
- Sonrisa's Butter Tart Squares
- Canadian Tea Biscuits
- Mushroom Bouchees

In desserts and beverages, there are several good options:
- Old-Fashioned Buttermilk Biscuits
- Maple Meringues
- Canadian Cocktail
- Classic Caesar
- Canadian Maple Old-Fashioned

Let's see other interesting Canadian meals in this cookbook that you can easily cook at home.

Canada

Canada isn't new to us! This North American state is known for its scenic beauty, cold weather, and amazing landscape. Canada is home to people belonging to many other countries; and for this reason, you you'll notice a diversity of cultures in this region. The country has ten provinces and three territories which are extended from the Atlantic Ocean to the Pacific and the Arctic Ocean. The country has an area 3,855.100 square miles (9,984,670 square kilometers), and that makes it the second-largest country by area in the world. It has the United States on its southern and western borders, and this border is known as the largest bi-national border in the world. Ottawa is the capital of the country, with Toronto, Montreal, and Vancouver as the three major metropolitan cities. Canada has several interesting sights to visit. Some of the major attractions in the country include the following:

- **Niagara Fall**

One of the most famous natural attractions in Canada is the popular Niagara fall. Millions of people visit each year to catch a glimpse of this massive fall extending up to 187 feet. There are several key points from where the tourist can watch this huge fall.

- **Banff National Park & the Rocky Mountains**

Banff National Park is located at the center of the Rocky Mountains in the province of Alberta, and it reflects some of the most beautiful scenery of Canada. There are beautiful Turquoise-colored lakes, amazing snow-capped peaks, and huge glaciers that are accessible in this park. The major attraction of the park is Lake Louise, which reflects the view of the surrounding glaciers and mountains. The visitors can walk around the shores. Moraine Lake is also located nearby, along with the famous Alpine Lark.

- **Old Quebec**

This place is now declared as one of Canada's historic gems by UNESCO. It covers the Upper and Lower Town of Quebec. The city's most historical buildings are located in this city. The Lower Town is situated along the St. Lawrence River. It was the home to the original settlement and to the Fairmont Le Château Frontenac. The Upper Town is located on 328 feet-high cliffs, and is home to the Plains of Abraham, the Citadel, Place d'Armes, and the Parque Historique de l'Artillerie.

My last visit to Canada delivered several amazing sights and an unforgettable experience of getting to know the Canadian food, the people, and the culture. The whole atmosphere is binding your mind and soul into it. So you'll love getting lost in the streets of Toronto and the Black Forest. If you too haven't been to Canada yet, then try its authentic meals and recipes from the cookbook and spread the traditional Canadian aromas all around you.

Breakfast

Pumpkin and Oat Pancakes

Preparation time: 10 minutes
Cook time: 10 minutes
Nutrition facts (per serving): 274 Cal (10g fat, 9g protein, 2.5g fiber)

Without these oat pancakes, it seems like the Canadian breakfast menu is incomplete. Try them with different variations of toppings.

Ingredients (4 servings)
1 cup all-purpose flour
1 cup quick-cooking oats
2 tablespoons toasted wheat germ
2 teaspoon sugar
2 teaspoon baking powder
½ teaspoon salt
Pinch ground cinnamon
⅔ cups whole milk
1 large egg, lightly beaten
¾ cup canned pumpkin
2 tablespoon canola oil

Preparation
Mix the cinnamon, salt, baking powder, sugar, wheat germ, oats and flour in a large bowl. Stir in the oil, pumpkin, egg, and milk and then mix evenly. Pour ¼ cup batter into a hot griddle and cook for 1-2 minutes per side. Cook more pancakes in the same way. Serve.

Buttermilk Pancakes

Preparation time: 10 minutes
Cook time: 8 minutes
Nutrition facts (per serving): 270 Cal (3g fat, 11g protein, 2g fiber)

This Canadian buttermilk pancakes are the everyday breakfast meal that you should definitely add to your menu. You can try these pancakes with eggs and crispy bacon.

Ingredients (4 servings)
4 cups all-purpose flour
¼ cup sugar
2 teaspoon baking soda
2 teaspoon salt
1 teaspoon baking powder
4 large eggs
4 cups buttermilk

Preparation
Whisk the salt, baking powder, baking soda, sugar, and flour in a large bowl. Beat in the buttermilk and the eggs and then mix well. Set a greased griddle over medium heat. Next, pour ¼ cup of the batter on to the griddle and cook for 1 minute per side. Serve.

Pumpkin Bread

Preparation time: 10 minutes
Cook time: 70 minutes
Nutrition facts (per serving): 202 Cal (7g fat, 6g protein, 1.3g fiber)

If you love to have a different variety of bread in your breakfast menu, then this pumpkin bread is a must to try with all the breakfast eggs, frittatas or bacon.

Ingredients (8 servings)
1 ⅔ cups all-purpose flour
1 ½ cups sugar
1 teaspoon baking soda
1 teaspoon ground cinnamon
¾ teaspoon salt
½ teaspoon baking powder
½ teaspoon ground nutmeg
¼ teaspoon ground cloves
2 large eggs
1 cup canned pumpkin
½ cup canola oil
½ cup water
½ cup walnuts, chopped
½ cup raisins

Preparation
At 350 degrees F, preheat your oven. Mix the pumpkin, eggs, and the rest of the ingredients in a bowl until smooth. Spread this prepared

mixture in a 9x5 inch greased loaf pan and bake for 70 minutes. Slice and serve.

Canadian Fried Dough

Preparation time: 15 minutes
Cook time: 8 minutes
Nutrition facts (per serving): 246 Cal (23g fat, 12g protein, 3g fiber)

This fried dough is another Canadian-inspired delight that you should definitely try on this cuisine. Serve with the flavorsome dips.

Ingredients (12 servings)

½ cup warm water
5 teaspoon active dry yeast
1 pinch white sugar
1 cup warm milk
⅓ cup white sugar
1½ teaspoon salt
1 teaspoon vanilla extract
3 beaten eggs
⅓ cup vegetable oil
5 cups whole-wheat flour
1-quart vegetable oil for frying
2 cups white sugar
½ teaspoon ground cinnamon

Preparation

Mix 1 pinch sugar, yeast, and warm water in a bowl and leave for 5 minutes. Stir in the eggs, ⅓ cup oil, vanilla extract, salt, milk and ⅓ cup sugar. Mix well, add the flour, and mix until smooth. Knead this prepared dough for 10 minutes. Roll the prepared dough into a ball, transfer it to a greased bowl then cover and leave for 1 hour. Knead the prepared dough and take a small egg-sized ball from this prepared dough and roll it out into ¼ inch thick round. Make more rounds in the same way. Set a deep-frying pan with cooking oil and heat it up to 375 degrees F. Deep fry the prepared dough in the hot oil until golden brown. Transfer the prepared dough to a plated lined with paper towel. Mix 2 cups sugar with cinnamon in a bowl. Drizzle cinnamon sugar over the prepared dough. Serve.

Cheddar-Ham Oven Omelet

Preparation time: 15 minutes
Cook time: 45 minutes
Nutrition facts (per serving): 208 Cal (14g fat, 15g protein, 4g fiber)

The famous ham oven omelet is essential on the Canadian breakfast menu. Try cooking it at home with these healthy ingredients and enjoy.

Ingredients (12 servings)
16 large eggs
2 cups whole milk
2 cups shredded cheddar cheese
¾ cup fully cooked ham, cubed
6 green onions, chopped

Preparation
At 350 degrees F, preheat your oven. Mix the eggs with the milk, onions, ham, and cheese in a bowl. Spread this prepared mixture in a 13x9 inch baking dish. Bake for 45 minutes. Slice and serve warm.

Cheddar Loaves

Preparation time: 10 minutes
Cook time: 40 minutes
Nutrition facts (per serving): 199 Cal (5g fat, 7g protein, 0g fiber)

The Canadian cheddar loaves are great to serve with all types of eggs meal and bacon. They have this appealing cheesy taste that goes with everything.

Ingredients (6 servings)

1 tablespoon active dry yeast

2 cups warm water

2 large eggs

2 tablespoon butter, softened

1 tablespoon sugar

2 teaspoon salt

7 ½ cups all-purpose flour

2 cups sharp cheddar cheese, shredded

Preparation

Whisk the yeast with warm water in a bowl and leave for 10 minutes. Stir in the flour, salt, sugar, butter, eggs, and milk and then mix until smooth. Knead this prepared dough on a floured surface for 8 minutes. Transfer the prepared dough to a greased bowl, cover, and leave for 1 hour. Punch down the prepared dough and stir in cheese. Divide this prepared dough in two- 6-inch loaf pans, cover, and leave the prepared dough for 45 minutes. At 350 degrees F, preheat your oven. Bake the bread for 40 minutes. Serve.

Sonrisa's Butter Tart Squares

Preparation time: 15 minutes
Cook time: 35 minutes
Nutrition facts (per serving): 220 Cal (10.4g fat, 2.4g protein, 18g fiber)

Have you tried the famous tart squares for breakfast? Well, here's a Canadian delight that adds pecans and raisins to your morning meal in a delicious way.

Ingredients (6 servings)
Base
1 cup all-purpose flour
¼ cup white sugar
½ cup cold butter

Topping
2 eggs, beaten
2 tablespoon melted butter
1 cup brown sugar
2 tablespoon all-purpose flour
½ teaspoon baking powder
½ teaspoon vanilla extract
1 cup raisins
½ cup chopped pecans

Preparation

At 350 degrees F, preheat your oven. Mix 1 cup flour, ½ cup cold butter and white sugar in a bowl until crumbly. Spread this prepared mixture in a 9-inch cake pan. Bake the crust for 15 minutes in the preheated oven. Allow the crust to cool. Beat the eggs with brown sugar, 2 tablespoon flour, vanilla, baking powder, and 2 tablespoon melted butter in a bowl. Stir in the pecans and raisins the then mix evenly. Spread this prepared mixture in the baked crust and bake again for 20 minutes. Allow the layers to cool and cut into squares. Serve.

Canadian Tea Biscuits

Preparation time: 15 minutes
Cook time: 15 minutes
Nutrition facts (per serving): 312 Cal (16g fat, 8g protein, 7g fiber)

The Canadian tea biscuits are famous for their delicious flavor and fluffy texture. Made from egg, flour, cheddar cheese and chives, these biscuits pair well with all the jams.

Ingredients (8 servings)
2 cups all-purpose flour
1 tablespoon baking powder
1 teaspoon salt
⅓ cup shortening
½ cup shredded Cheddar cheese
2 tablespoon chopped fresh chives
1 cup milk

Preparation
At 425 degrees F, preheat your oven. Mix baking powder, salt, and flour in a bowl. Stir in the shortening and mix until crumbly. Add the chives and the cheddar cheese and then make soft dough. Knead this prepared dough on the working surface and roll out into 1-inch thick sheet. Cut the prepared dough into 2 ½ inch round biscuits using a cookie cutter. Place the cookies on the baking sheet and bake for 15 minutes. Serve.

Browned Butter Banana Bread

Preparation time: 10 minutes
Cook time: 45 minutes
Nutrition facts (per serving): 378 Cal (16g fat, 4g protein, 2g fiber)

This Canadian banana bread tastes heavenly when cooked and baked at home. Serve warm with your favorite egg meal on the side.

Ingredients (6 servings)

½ cup butter
3 very ripe bananas
¼ cup brown sugar
¼ cup white sugar
1 egg
1 tablespoon vanilla extract
1½ cups all-purpose flour
1½ teaspoons baking soda
1 teaspoon ground cinnamon
½ teaspoon ground nutmeg

Preparation

Cook the butter in a saucepan on a low simmer for 10 minutes. Allow the butter to cool and use ⅓ cup browned butter. At 350 degrees F, preheat your oven. Grease a loaf pan with cooking oil. Mash 3 peeled bananas in a large bowl and stir in ⅓ cup brown butter, vanilla extract, egg, white sugar, and brown sugar. Mix well then add nutmeg, cinnamon, baking soda, and flour then mix evenly. Spread this prepared mixture in a greased pan and bake for 45 minutes. Allow the bread to cool.

Easter Hot Cross Buns

Preparation time: 15 minutes
Cook time: 12 minutes
Nutrition facts (per serving): 256 Cal (16g fat, 11g protein, 6g fiber)

Canadian cross buns are another nutritious yet simple meal for the breakfast table. It adds lots of nutrients and fibers to the table, along with healthy ingredients, that are cooked together in a tempting combination.

Ingredients (8 servings)
¾ cup lukewarm milk
1 (¼ oz.) package active dry yeast
1 teaspoon white sugar
3 ¼ cups all-purpose flour
¼ cup white sugar
1 teaspoon salt
½ teaspoon ground cinnamon
½ teaspoon ground allspice
¼ teaspoon ground cloves
¼ teaspoon ground nutmeg
¼ cup softened butter
2 large eggs
¾ cup golden raisins, chopped
2 tablespoon orange marmalade

Glaze

1 egg white

1 tablespoon milk

Frosting

⅓ cup confectioners' sugar

1 ½ teaspoon milk

Preparation

Mix 1 teaspoon sugar, yeast and ¼ cup milk in a bowl and leave for 5 minutes. Stir in 3 cups flour, nutmeg, cloves, allspice, cinnamon, salt, butter, eggs, ½ cup milk, and ¼ cup white sugar. Next, mix well into smooth dough. Knead this prepared dough on a floured surface and leave for 10 minutes. Place the prepared dough in a greased bowl, cover and leave for 2 hours. Punch down the prepared dough and divide into 16 pieces. Roll the prepared dough into buns and place them in the baking sheets. Cover and leave for 40 minutes. At 400 degrees F, preheat your oven. Beat the egg whites with 1 tablespoon milk in a small bowl. Cut a large cross on top of each bun and brush them with the egg wash. Bake the buns for 12 minutes then allow them to cool. Serve.

Mushroom Bouchees

Preparation time: 15 minutes
Cook time: 20 minutes
Nutrition facts (per serving): 410 Cal (6g fat, 20g protein, 1.4g fiber)

Try these mushroom Bouchees for your breakfast, and you'll soon forget about the rest. The recipe is simple and gives you lots of nutrients in one place.

Ingredients (6 servings)
Cooking spray
3 green onions
1 (10 oz.) can mushroom pieces, drained
2 tablespoon butter
2 tablespoon cornstarch
½ cup half-and-half
Salt and black pepper to taste
1 pinch garlic powder, or to taste
10 slices sandwich bread

Preparation
At 350 degrees F, preheat your oven. Layer a baking sheet with cooking spray. First, chop the mushrooms and green onions in a food processor. Sauté the mushrooms and onions with in a small saucepan for 2 minutes. Mix the cornstarch with half and half in a bowl. Pour the mixture over the mushrooms then cook for 3 minutes. Stir in the garlic powder, black pepper, and salt. Cut the bread into 1-inch thick round and place them in a baking sheet. Bake the bread for 10 minutes until brown. Spread the mushroom mixture on top. Serve.

Slow Cooker Western Omelets Brunch Bake

Preparation time: 15 minutes
Cook time: 3 hours 7 minutes
Nutrition facts (per serving): 226 Cal (24g fat, 4g protein, 1g fiber)

The famous brunch bake is one of the Canadian specialties, and everyone must try this interesting combination of different toppings.

Ingredients (6 servings)
1 tablespoon butter
1 onion, diced
1 small red sweet pepper, diced
1 small yellow pepper, diced
4 cups frozen hash brown potatoes
1 cup cooked ham, diced
6 large eggs
2 tablespoon cream
1 teaspoon dry mustard
1 teaspoon garlic powder
½ teaspoon salt
Pinch cayenne pepper
1 cup cheddar cheese, shredded

Preparation
Sauté the onion, yellow peppers, and butter in a large skillet for 7 minutes and then transfer this prepared mixture to a slow cooker. Add

the ham and the potatoes. Beat the garlic powder, cayenne, salt, mustard, cream, and eggs in a bowl and pour over the veggies in the slow cooker. Drizzle the cheese on top and cover. Cook on High heat for 3 hours. Slice and serve.

Partridgeberry Banana Pancakes

Preparation time: 15 minutes
Cook time: 4 minutes
Nutrition facts (per serving): 211 Cal (17g fat, 6g protein, 0.7g fiber)

These banana pancakes are the best way to enjoy soft and savory bread in the morning in the Canadian style. Serve with freshly cooked eggs.

Ingredients (4 servings)
Dry
½ cup buckwheat flour
½ cup brown rice flour
2 tablespoon arrowroot flour
1 teaspoon cinnamon
1 teaspoon baking powder
1 pinch of sea salt

Wet
1 egg
½ tablespoon vanilla
¾ cup almond milk or water

Add-ons
¼ cup partridgeberries
½ banana, sliced
Coconut oil to grease pan

Preparation

Mix all the flours and the wet ingredients in a bowl then mix well. Fold in the banana and the berries and then mix evenly. Place a suitable skillet over medium low heat and grease with cooking oil. Pour ½ cup batter into the skillet and cook for 2 minutes per side. Cook more pancakes in the same way. Drizzle maple syrup on top and serve.

Breakfast Poutine

Preparation time: 10 minutes
Cook time: 14 minutes
Nutrition facts (per serving): 217 Cal (14g fat, 9g protein, 0.3g fiber)

This breakfast poutine is a perfect morning meal! Keep it ready in the refrigerator to serve with your favorite sauce on top. It's super-rich, healthy, and delicious.

Ingredients (6 servings)

1 cup pieces, thick cut bacon
½ tablespoon garlic powder
¼ teaspoon sea salt
½ teaspoon chili powder
½ teaspoon mustard powder
¼ teaspoon onion powder
2 ½ cups julienned Russet potato skin on
1 cup vegetable oil
2 tablespoon fresh parsley, chopped
1 cup grated Cheddar cheese
4 eggs poached

Maple Hollandaise Sauce

¼ cup butter
2 eggs
1 tablespoon pure maple syrup
1 tablespoon fresh lemon juice
Pinch smoked paprika

Preparation

Sauté the bacon in a skillet for 8 minutes until crispy. Mix the onion powder, mustard powder, chili powder, salt and garlic powder in a small bowl. Add the oil to a deep stock pot and heat to 375 degrees F. Deep fry the potatoes until golden and then transfer to a suitable plate lined with baking sheet. Sprinkle the spices mixture and the parsley on top and toss well. Beat the eggs with lemon juice and maple syrup in a bowl. Stir in the melted butter and beat for 6 minutes. Spread the fries on two plates. Pour the hollandaise sauce over the fries. Drizzle bacon and cheese on top. Add 2 poached eggs and garnish with paprika and parsley. Serve.

Coconut and Flaxseed Toast

Preparation time: 15 minutes
Cook time: 10 minutes
Nutrition facts (per serving): 242 Cal (8g fat, 2g protein, 1g fiber)

If you haven't tried the Canadian toasts before, then here comes a simple and easy to cook recipe that you can prepare at home in no time with minimum efforts.

Ingredients (6 servings)
1 egg
1 tablespoon vanilla Greek yogurt
1 tablespoon shredded coconut unsweetened
1 ½ teaspoon flaxseeds
1 teaspoon vanilla extract
1 teaspoon coconut oil
2 slices whole grain loaf
¼ cup blackberries
½ cup blueberries
½ cup raspberries
Pure maple syrup

Preparation
Beat the egg with the yogurt, vanilla, flaxseeds, and coconut in a bowl. Spread the coconut oil in a skillet and melt over low heat. Dip the bread in the yogurt mixture and sear for 3 minutes per side. Garnish with maple syrup and berries. Serve.

Montreal Bagels

Preparation time: 10 minutes
Cook time: 20 minutes
Nutrition facts (per serving): 301 Cal (3g fat, 4g protein, 4g fiber)

How about some delicious Montreal bagels? Have you ever tried making these bagels at home? If you haven't, now is the time to cook them using simple and healthy ingredients.

Ingredients (6 servings)
1 cup lukewarm water
2 teaspoon pure maple syrup
2 teaspoon active dry yeast
3 ¼ cups bread flour
1 teaspoon salt
¾ cup sesame seeds
⅓ cup honey

Preparation
Mix the lukewarm water, yeast, and maple syrup in a bowl. Leave the mixture for 5 minutes. Stir in the flour, salt, and honey and then mix well until smooth. Divide this prepared dough into 8 pieces and roll each into a round. Cut a hole at the center of each round. Place the bagels on a baking sheet, drizzle sesame seeds on top, cover, and leave for 1 ½ hours. Bake for 20 minutes at 475 degrees F. Allow the bagels to cool. Serve.

Appetizers

Canadian Bacon Cheese Straws

Preparation time: 15 minutes
Cook time: 13 minutes
Nutrition facts (per serving): 230 Cal (22g fat, 10g protein, 1.4g fiber)

If you haven't tried the Canadian cheese straws before, then here comes a simple and easy to cook recipe that you can easily prepare and cook at home in no time with minimum efforts.

Ingredients (10 servings)
1 sheet puff pastry store-bought, thawed
½ cup Parmesan cheese grated
½ cup Gruyere cheese, grated
½ cup Canadian bacon, minced
⅛ teaspoon cayenne pepper
¼ teaspoon coarse salt or sea salt
⅛ teaspoon black pepper
1 teaspoon poppy seeds
Fresh herbs parsley, basil, rosemary, minced
Honey mustard sauce, for dipping

Preparation

At 425 degrees F, preheat your oven. Layer 2 baking sheets with baking paper. Mix the cayenne pepper, cheese, and Parmesan in a small bowl. Spread this cheese mixture on a working surface and add the puff paste. Roll out the prepared dough into a 10x13 inches rectangle. Top the prepared dough with the minced ham, salt, and poppy seeds, fold the prepared dough, and press to seal the filling. Cut the prepared dough into ¾ inch strips. Twist the strips into a straw. Place the cheesy straws on a baking tray and allow it cool for 15 minutes. Bake the straws for 13 minutes in the oven until golden brown. Serve.

Creamy Caramel Dip

Preparation time: 15 minutes
Nutrition facts (per serving): 87 Cal (5g fat, 1g protein, 5g fiber)

If you haven't tried the creamy caramel dip recipe before, then here comes a simple and easy to cook recipe that you prep with minimum efforts.

Ingredients (8 servings)
1 package (8 oz.) cream cheese, softened
¾ cup packed brown sugar
1 cup sour cream
2 teaspoon vanilla extract
2 teaspoon lemon juice
1 cup cold milk
1 package (3.4 oz.) instant vanilla pudding mix
Assorted fresh fruit

Preparation
Mix the cream cheese with the brown sugar in a bowl until smooth. Stir in the pudding mix, milk, lemon juice, vanilla, and sour cream and then mix well. Cover and refrigerate the prepared dip for 1 hour. Serve.

Cheddar Pan Rolls

Preparation time: 10 minutes
Cook time: 25 minutes
Nutrition facts (per serving): 425 Cal (28g fat, 33g protein, 2g fiber)

Have you tried the Canadian pan rolls before? Well, now you can enjoy this unique and flavorsome combination by cooking this recipe on your own.

Ingredients (6 servings)
4 ½ cups all-purpose flour
2 tablespoon sugar
1 tablespoon salt
1 package (¼ oz.) active dry yeast
2 cups milk
1 tablespoon butter
2 cups cheddar cheese, shredded
1 large egg white, beaten

Preparation
Mix the yeast, salt, sugar, and 2 cups of flour in a large bowl. Warm the milk with butter in a small saucepan to 120 degrees F. Remove it from the heat, stir in the dry ingredients, and then mix well to make soft dough. Cover this prepared dough and leave for 45 minutes. Punch down the prepared dough and divide into 3 portions. Make 12 balls from each portion. Grease 3- 9-inch baking pans with cooking oil and place the prepared dough balls in the pans. Cover and leave for 30

minutes. Brush the balls with the egg white and bake for 25 minutes at 350 degrees F until golden brown. Serve.

Air-Fryer Crispy Sriracha Spring Rolls

Preparation time: 15 minutes
Cook time: 26 minutes
Nutrition facts (per serving): 289 Cal (13g fat, 3g protein, 2g fiber)

It's about time to try the crispy spring rolls with some delicious tomato sauce on the side. Now you can cook them in an air fryer.

Ingredients (8 servings)
3 cups coleslaw mix
3 green onions, chopped
1 tablespoon soy sauce
1 teaspoon sesame oil
1 pound boneless chicken breasts
1 teaspoon seasoned salt
2 packages (8 oz.) cream cheese, softened
2 tablespoon Sriracha chili sauce
24 spring roll wrappers
Cooking spray
Sweet chili sauce and green onions

Preparation
At 360 degrees F, preheat your oven. Mix the sesame oil, soy sauce, green onion, and the coleslaw mix in a bowl. Place the chicken in the greased air fryer basket and air fry for 20 minutes. Remove the chicken from the air fryer and cut into cubes. Mix the chili sauce, cream cheese, chicken, and the coleslaw mixture in a bowl. Place a roll wrapper on the working surface, add 2 tablespoon of chicken filling on top of 1 corner of the

wrappers, and then roll to make a roll. Repeat the same steps with the remaining wrappers and filling. Place the rolls in the air fryer basket, spray them with cooking oil, and air fry for 6 minutes. Serve with the sweet chili sauce and the green onions.

Authentic Canadian Poutine

Preparation time: 10 minutes
Cook time: 15 minutes
Nutrition facts (per serving): 162 Cal (13g fat, 15g protein, 2g fiber)

If you can't think of anything to cook and make in a short time, then try this authentic poutine as the perfect choice because it has a great taste and amazing texture to serve at the table.

Ingredients (6 servings)
Poutine Gravy
3 tablespoon cornstarch
2 tablespoon water
6 tablespoon unsalted butter
¼ cup all-purpose flour
20 oz. beef broth
10 oz. chicken broth
Pepper, to taste
2 lbs. Russet potatoes
Peanut oil
1 ½ cups white cheddar cheese curds

Preparation
Mix the cornstarch with water in a bowl. Sauté the flour with the melted butter in a large saucepan for 5 minutes until golden brown. Stir in the broth and mix well until smooth. Stir in the cornstarch mixture and cook until the mixture thickens. Add the black pepper and salt; then mix well. Meanwhile, cut the potatoes into ½ inch thick strips. Soak the

potatoes in cold water in a bowl. Leave for 1 hour then drain. Heat oil in a deep-frying pan at 300 degrees F. Pat dry the potatoes and deep fry them for almost 8 minutes until golden brown. Transfer the potatoes to a plate lined with a paper towel. Toss the fries with salt in a bowl and pour the gravy over the fries. Add the cheese curds and the black pepper on top. Serve.

Cheese Spread

Preparation time: 15 minutes
Cook time: 1 minute
Nutrition facts (per serving): 357 Cal (32g fat, 15g protein, 1.4g fiber)

Try this Canadian cheese spread on the menu. The combination of cream cheese with sharp cheddar cheese and onion is bliss for all cheese lovers like me.

Ingredients (8 servings)

1 (8 ounce) package cream cheese
1 (8 ounce) container sharp Cheddar cheese
¼ cup red onion, chopped
1 tablespoon Worcestershire sauce
2 teaspoons black pepper
1 teaspoon paprika
1 dash hot sauce, or to taste

Preparation

Heat the cream cheese in a bowl in a microwave for 1 minute and then add the cheese, red onion, Worcestershire sauce, black pepper, paprika, and hot sauce. Mix well and serve.

Mushroom and Bannock Bites

Preparation time: 15 minutes
Cook time: 43 minutes
Nutrition facts (per serving): 206 Cal (29g fat, 4g protein, 0.1g fiber)

The appetizing bannock bites makes a great addition to the menu, and they look magical when served at the table.

Ingredients (8 servings)
3 cups all-purpose flour
2 tablespoon baking powder
½ teaspoon salt
1 pinch of sugar
¼ cup butter
¼ cup vegetable shortening
¾ cup water

Mushroom Gravy
¼ cup canola oil
¼ cup yellow onion, chopped
1 cup Cremini mushrooms, chopped
1 cup White Button mushrooms chopped
½ teaspoon salt
¼ cup Canadian Whiskey
½ cup vegetable broth
½ teaspoon dried thyme
¼ teaspoon black pepper

Sautéed Mushrooms

⅛ cup canola oil

10 Cremini mushrooms, sliced

10 White Button mushrooms, sliced

½ teaspoon salt

Preparation

At 425 degrees F, preheat your oven. Mix the flour with the salt, sugar, and baking powder in a mixing bowl. Stir in the shortening and the butter and then mix until crumbly. Stir in ¼ cup water and then mix until smooth. Spread the prepared dough in a greased baking sheet and bake for 25 minutes. Sauté the mushrooms with canola oil, onion and salt in a saucepan for 8 minutes. Stir in the whiskey, spices, and broth and then cook for 5 minutes. Blend this cooked mixture until smooth. Remove the baked bannock from the heat and cut into squares.

For the sautéed mushrooms, add the salt, mushrooms, and canola oil to a skillet then sauté for 5 minutes until golden brown. Place the bannock bread squares on a plate, pour the mushroom sauce on top, and add the sautéed mushrooms on top. Serve.

Classic Canadian Butter Tarts

Preparation time: 15 minutes
Cook time: 15 minutes
Nutrition facts (per serving): 279 Cal (5.2g fat, 2.8g protein, 3g fiber)

If you haven't tried the Canadian butter tarts, then you now as they have no parallel in taste and texture.

Ingredients (6 servings)
Pastry
2 ¼ cups flour
1 tablespoon brown sugar
½ teaspoon salt
½ cup shortening
½ cup butter
6 tablespoon ice water

Filling
½ cup brown sugar
½ cup corn syrup
¼ cup butter, melted
1 egg
1 teaspoon vanilla extract
¼ teaspoon salt
½ cup raisins

Preparation

Blend the cold butter, shortening, flour, sugar, and water in a food process until it makes smooth dough. Divide the prepared dough into two rounds and wrap them in a plastic wrap. Refrigerate the prepared dough for 30 minutes. Roll each dough half into ½ inch thick sheet and cut into 4-inch rounds using a cookie cutter. Place one round in each muffin cup of a tray and press it with a finger. Refrigerate the pastry crust for 1 hour. Meanwhile, mix all the filling ingredients, except the raisins, in a bowl. Divide the raisins in the crusts and top them with the prepared filling. Bake the tarts for 15 minutes at 425 degrees F. Allow the tarts to cool and serve.

Pea Meal Bacon

Preparation time: 15 minutes
Cook time: 3 hours 35 minutes
Nutrition facts (per serving): 232 Cal (11g fat, 23g protein, 3g fiber)

This pea meal bacon is one popular Canadian delight to serve on the menu. It's also quick to make if you have pork loin at home.

Ingredients (8 servings)
1 pork loin (about 4 lbs.), diced
12 cups cold water
1 cup maple syrup
½ cup pickling salt
2 teaspoon Prague cure
2 tablespoon mustard seeds
2 teaspoon black peppercorns
4 garlic cloves pressed
3 whole cloves
2 bay leaves
1 lemon sliced into wedges

Preparation
Boil 4 cups water and the remaining spices in a saucepan for 5 minutes. Remove it from the heat, add the pork loin, cover, and leave the pork for 5 days for curing. Drain and pat dry the pork loin. Coat the pork loin with the cornmeal. Set a grill over 225 degrees F and place the pork loin in the grill. Cover and smoke for 3 ½ hours. Slice and serve.

Grilled Oysters

Preparation time: 15 minutes
Cook time: 6 minutes
Nutrition facts (per serving): 146 Cal (21g fat, 9g protein, 4.1g fiber)

These grilled oysters are everyone's favorite go-to meal when it comes to serving Canadian meals; you can prepare it in no time.

Ingredients (16 servings)

16 oysters

Tabasco sauce

1 lemon, cut into wedges

Chopped parsley, to taste

Preparation

Set a grill over medium-high heat. Place the oysters on the grill and cook for 6 minutes. Split the oysters in half and remove their top shells. Mix each oyster with the parsley, lemon juice, and tabasco. Serve.

Cinnamon-Sugar Snowshoes

Preparation time: 10 minutes
Cook time: 12 minutes
Nutrition facts (per serving): 172 Cal (5g fat, 1.4g protein, 2g fiber)

Canadian snowshoes are another great side serving for the table, and you can offer them as a delicious and healthy snack meal as well.

Ingredients (8 servings)
¾ cup milk
1 teaspoon active dry yeast
1 ¾ cups all-purpose flour
2 tablespoon butter, melted
¼ teaspoon salt
Cinnamon sugar
⅔ cup granulated sugar
2 teaspoon cinnamon
¼ cup butter, melted
Lemon wedges, optional

Preparation
Mix the warm milk with the yeast in a bowl and leave for 5 minutes. Stir in the salt, 2 tablespoon of butter, and flour; then mix well for 5 minutes. Transfer the bowl to a greased bowl, cover and leave for 1 hour. Spread the parchment paper on a greased baking sheet. Punch down the prepared dough then divide it into 8 portions. Place the portions in the baking sheet, cover with a damp tea towel and leave for 15 minutes. Roll out each dough ball into ⅛ in thick oval. Add the ovals

to the prepared baking sheets, cover, and leave for 15 minutes. Add the oil to a deep-frying pan and heat it to 325 degrees F. fry each dough pieces in the oil for 3 minutes then transfer to a plate, lined with paper towel. Mix the sugar with cinnamon in a bowl. Brush the prepared dough with the butter and drizzle the cinnamon sugar on top. Serve.

Maple-Fennel Bacon

Preparation time: 10 minutes
Cook time: 35 minutes
Nutrition facts (per serving): 102 Cal (5g fat, 5g protein, 2g fiber)

Here's is another most popular snack in Canadian Cuisine, and it has this great taste from the mix of maple and brown sugar.

Ingredients (12 servings)
12 slices bacon
3 tablespoon maple syrup
2 teaspoon brown sugar
1 teaspoon fennel seeds

Preparation
At 375 degrees F, preheat your oven. Layer a baking sheet with a foil sheet. Place the bacon over the oven rack. Mix the sugar and the maple syrup in a bowl. Brush this prepared mixture over the bacon. Drizzle the fennel seeds and the black pepper over the bacon. Bake the bacon for 35 minutes in the oven. Serve.

Salads

Fennel Salad with Citrus Dressing

Preparation time: 15 minutes
Nutrition facts (per serving): 160 Cal (15g fat, 1g protein, 2g fiber)

The Canadian fennel salad is famous for its texture, unique taste, and aroma. So now you can bring those exotic flavors home by using this recipe.

Ingredients (4 servings)
1 large fennel bulb, sliced
1 small apple, sliced
¼ cup sweet onion, sliced

Dressing
⅓ cup olive oil
½ teaspoon grated lemon zest
2 tablespoon lemon juice
½ teaspoon grated orange zest
2 tablespoon orange juice
½ teaspoon Dijon mustard
½ teaspoon salt
⅛ teaspoon black pepper

Preparation
Mix the fennel, apple, sweet onion, and the rest of the dressing ingredients in a bowl. Serve.

Canadian Pub Salad

Preparation time: 10 minutes
Nutrition facts (per serving): 211 Cal (20g fat, 4g protein, 13g fiber)

This dish is the right fit to serve with all your Canadian entrees. Here the lettuce and green beans are mixed with other veggies to make an amazing combination.

Ingredients (6 servings)
½ package (14 oz.) coleslaw mix
2 cups Brussels sprouts, sliced
1 ½ cups baby kale, chopped
½ cup golden raisins
½ cup dried cranberries

Dressing
⅓ cup canola oil
2 tablespoon white wine vinegar
1 teaspoon whole grain mustard
1 tablespoon maple syrup

Preparation
Mix the coleslaw mix with the rest of the ingredients in a salad bowl. Serve.

Canadian Caesar Salad

Preparation time: 10 minutes
Nutrition facts (per serving): 253 Cal (2g fat, 1g protein, 4g fiber)

This Caesar salad is a delicious and healthy salad, which has a refreshing taste due to the use of herbs and spices in it. It's great to serve with skewers.

Ingredients (6 servings)
2 garlic cloves, chopped
¼ teaspoon salt
1 tablespoon drained capers
2 teaspoon anchovy paste
½ cup olive oil
¼ teaspoon black pepper
1 ½ teaspoon Worcestershire sauce
1 teaspoon distilled white vinegar
½ teaspoon prepared hot mustard
4 dashes hot pepper sauce
2 egg yolks
½ lemon, juiced
1 head romaine lettuce, torn
¼ cup real bacon bits, or to taste
1 (5 oz.) package croutons
4 teaspoon Parmesan cheese, grated

Preparation
Mix the capers with the rest of the ingredients in a salad bowl. Serve.

Tomato and Orzo Summer Salad

Preparation time: 10 minutes
Nutrition facts (per serving): 179 Cal (16g fat, 15g protein, 3g fiber)

The Canadian orzo salad is a special fresh veggie salad, and it's a must to serve with all the different entrees. Use this quick and simple recipe to get it ready in no time.

Ingredients (6 servings)
1 garlic clove, minced
¼ cup olive oil
¼ cup red wine vinegar
1 teaspoon liquid honey
1 teaspoon salt
¼ teaspoon pepper
½ cup thinly sliced red onion
1 cup orzo, cooked
1 English cucumber, cut in ¼-inch thick slices
1 heirloom tomato, cut in wedges
2 cups cherry tomatoes, halved
½ cup basil leaves, torn
½ cup crumbled feta cheese

Preparation
Mix the orzo with the rest of the ingredients in a salad bowl. Serve.

Chicken Waldorf Wedge Salad

Preparation time: 10 minutes
Nutrition facts (per serving): 276 Cal (17g fat, 7g protein, 3g fiber)

It's truly as if the Canadian menu is incomplete without this Waldorf salad. It's made from lettuce, chicken, and blue cheese, which add lots of nutritional value to this salad.

Ingredients (6 servings)

1 garlic clove, minced
1 cup Greek yogurt
⅓ cup chopped parsley
⅓ cup olive oil
8 teaspoon lemon juice
½ teaspoon salt
2 ribs celery, trimmed, ribs chopped
1 peach, cut in 1-inch chunks
2 cups cooked boneless chicken breast, chopped
1 ½ cup red grapes, halved
4 rounds (1 inch thick) iceberg lettuce
1 cup walnuts, toasted and chopped
½ cup crumbled blue cheese

Preparation

Mix the yogurt with the rest of the ingredients in a salad bowl, except for the cabbage. Place the cabbage rounds on a serving plate and spread the yogurt mixture on top. Serve.

Macaroni Salad

Preparation time: 10 minutes
Nutrition facts (per serving): 155 Cal (8g fat, 3g protein, 2g fiber)

If you haven't tried this macaroni salad before, then here comes a simple and easy to cook recipe that you can recreate at home in no time with minimum efforts.

Ingredients (6 servings)
1 carrot, chopped
Half small onion, chopped
½ cup cider vinegar
3 tablespoon granulated sugar
1 teaspoon salt
4 cups elbow macaroni, boiled
3 green onions, chopped
1 jar diced pimiento peppers, drained
1 ¼ cup mayonnaise
¾ teaspoon black pepper

Preparation
Mix the boiled macaroni with the rest of the ingredients in a salad bowl. Serve.

Avocado and Grilled Corn Salad

Preparation time: 10 minutes
Nutrition facts (per serving): 243 Cal (13g fat, 5g protein, 2g fiber)

Here's one recipe that everyone tries on this menu. It's made with grilled corn cobs and avocado.

Ingredients (6 servings)
Dressing
1 small garlic clove, minced
6 tablespoon olive oil
1 ½ teaspoon lime zest
¼ cup lime juice
4 teaspoon liquid honey
¾ teaspoon salt

Salad
3 corncobs, husked
1 tablespoon olive oil
2 avocados, sliced
⅓ cup red onion, sliced
½ cup shaved Parmesan cheese
¼ cup mint, chopped
¼ cup parsley, chopped
1 pinch salt

Preparation
Mix the grilled corn with the rest of the ingredients in a salad bowl. Serve.

Grilled Peach and Tomato Salad

Preparation time: 15 minutes
Cook time: 4 minutes
Nutrition facts (per serving): 381 Cal (5g fat, 3g protein, 6g fiber)

If you haven't tried this grilled peach salad before, then here comes a simple and easy to cook recipe that you can recreate at home in no time with minimum efforts.

Ingredients (6 servings)
Dressing
2 tablespoon white balsamic vinegar
½ cup thinly sliced red onion
3 tablespoon olive oil
2 teaspoon grainy mustard
1 teaspoon liquid honey
¼ teaspoon salt
¼ teaspoon pepper

Salad
2 peaches, pitted and quartered
1 teaspoon olive oil
1 lb. mixed heirloom tomatoes, chopped
1 cup sliced sugar snap peas
¼ cup chopped fresh mint
2 tablespoon chopped fresh tarragon
¼ cup crumbled feta cheese

Preparation

Set a grill over high heat and grill the peaches for 2 minutes per side. Mix the grilled peaches with the rest of the ingredients in a salad bowl. Serve.

Fennel and Radicchio Salad

Preparation time: 15 minutes
Nutrition facts (per serving): 252 Cal (13g fat, 24g protein, 4g fiber)

The Canadian fennel and radicchio salad is a pure delight to serve with all entrees. It's known for its comforting effects, and the meal offers a very energizing combination of ingredients.

Ingredients (6 servings)
1 head red leaf lettuce, torn
1 head radicchio, torn
Half bulb fennel, cored and sliced
2 cups cress
½ cup green onion vinaigrette
¼ teaspoon salt
¼ cup pepitas

Preparation
Mix the lettuce with the rest of the ingredients in a salad bowl. Serve.

Canadian Cobb Salad

Preparation time: 10 minutes
Cook time: 37 minutes
Nutrition facts (per serving): 260 Cal (3g fat, 3g protein, 11g fiber)

Try this Canadian Cobb salad with your favorite herbs on top. Adding a dollop of cream or yogurt will make it even richer in taste.

Ingredients (4 servings)
2 chicken breasts, cut in half horizontally
6 slices of bacon
Salt, to taste
Freshly ground pepper, to taste
1 teaspoon paprika
3 eggs
3 tablespoon red wine vinegar
¼ cup canola oil
3 tablespoon fresh chives chopped
6 cups mixed lettuce
2 avocados cut into wedges
2 tomatoes cut into wedges
5 oz. Canadian Blue cheese cut into cubes

Preparation
At 425 degrees F, preheat your oven. Rub the chicken with the black pepper, salt, and paprika. Spread the chicken and bacon on a baking sheet lined with parchment paper. Bake the chicken for 15 minutes. Transfer the chicken to a suitable plate and continue cooking the bacon

until crispy. Boil the eggs with water for 12 minutes, drain, and peel them. Mix the black pepper, salt, chives, oil, and vinegar in a jar. Cut the chicken into strips, chop the bacons, and cut eggs into quarters. Toss all the ingredients in a baking sheet and drizzle the prepared dressing on top. Serve.

Soups

Canadian Cheese Soup

Preparation time: 10 minutes
Cook time: 25 minutes
Nutrition facts (per serving): 361 Cal (14g fat, 2g protein, 2g fiber)

Enjoy this Canadian cheese soup recipe with mixed potatoes flavors. Adding cream or sour cream on top delivers a very distinctive taste to the soup.

Ingredients (6 servings)
3 cups chicken broth
4 medium potatoes, peeled and diced
2 celery ribs, diced
1 medium carrot, diced
1 small onion, diced
6 oz. Canadian bacon, trimmed and diced
2 tablespoon butter
2 tablespoon all-purpose flour
1 cup whole milk
2 cups cheddar cheese, shredded
⅛ teaspoon black pepper

Preparation
Add the broth, potatoes, celery, carrot, and onion to a deep pan and then cook for 20 minutes on a simmer. Lightly mash the potatoes and then add bacon. Sauté the flour with the butter in a skillet for 1 minute. Stir in the milk and cook the mixture to a boil while mixing. Cook for 2

minutes and then add to the vegetable mixture. Stir in the black pepper and the cheese. Finally, cook until melted. Serve warm.

Cream of Celery Soup with Seared Scallops

Preparation time: 10 minutes
Cook time: 30 minutes
Nutrition facts (per serving): 310 Cal (11g fat, 22g protein, 6g fiber)

Make this Canadian basic celery soup in no time and enjoy it with some garnish on top. Adding a drizzle of paprika on top makes it super tasty.

Ingredients (4 servings)
2 onions, chopped
4 cloves garlic, chopped
2 tablespoon olive oil
5 cups chopped celery
2 potatoes, peeled and cubed
5 cups chicken broth
¼ cup heavy cream
Salt and black pepper, to taste

Spinach Cream
5 cups fresh spinach
½ cup heavy cream

Scallops
12 frozen scallops, patted dry
2 tablespoon olive oil
Zest of 1 lemon
Fresh chervil leaves

Preparation

Sauté the onions with celery, garlic, and oil in a deep pot for 2 minutes. Stir in the potatoes and the broth and then cook to a boil. Cover and cook for 20 minutes on a simmer. Puree this soup, add the salt, cream, and black pepper. Boil the cream and the spinach in a pan for 3 minutes and then blend with the black pepper and the salt in a blender. Sauté the scallops with oil in a skillet for 2 minutes per side. Add the black pepper and the salt. Divide the cream of celery soup in the serving bowls and top each with green mixture and scallops. Garnish with lemon and chervil leaves. Serve.

Cream of Parsnip Soup with Broccoli and Cranberries

Preparation time: 15 minutes
Cook time: 30 minutes
Nutrition facts (per serving): 417 Cal (2g fat, 23 protein, 2g fiber)

Cream of Parsnip Soup is also quite famous in the region; in fact, it's a staple because of its nutritional content.

Ingredients (4 servings)
Cream of Parsnip Soup
1 onion, chopped
2 tablespoon butter
2.2 lb. parsnips, peeled and sliced
4 cups chicken broth
2 cups milk
Salt and black pepper, to taste

Topping
1 small broccoli, cut
½ lb. ground venison, caribou or bison
1 garlic clove, chopped
¼ cup (60 ml) olive oil
2 tablespoon dried cranberries, chopped
2 tablespoon grated Parmigiano-Reggiano cheese

Preparation

Sauté the onions with the butter in a deep pot for 2minutes. Stir in the parsnips, milk, and broth and then cook to a boil. Cover and cook for 25 minutes on a simmer. Puree this soup and then add the salt and the black pepper. Sauté the broccoli florets with 1 tablespoon oil in a skillet for 1 minute. Divide the cream of parsnip soup in the serving bowls and top each with broccoli. Garnish with meat, Parmesan, and cranberries. Serve.

Ontario Butternut Squash Soup

Preparation time: 10 minutes
Cook time: 45 minutes
Nutrition facts (per serving): 180 Cal (4g fat, 15g protein, 3g fiber)

This Ontario soup is everything I was looking for. The butternut squash, curry powder, and cream make a complete package for a health enthusiast like me.

Ingredients (6 servings)

2 onions, chopped
2 garlic cloves, chopped
1 tablespoon fresh ginger, peeled and chopped
2 tablespoon olive oil
5 cups butternut squash, peeled, and diced
2 tablespoon mild curry powder
1 teaspoon dry mustard
5 cups chicken broth
1 tablespoon heavy cream
Cilantro leaves, to garnish
Hot peppers, thinly sliced
Salt and black pepper, to taste

Preparation

Sauté the onion, garlic, ginger, and oil in a skillet until soft. Stir in the buttercup squash and sauté for 5 minutes. Add the rest of the soup ingredients, mix well, and cook until the squash is soft. Puree the cooked soup and serve warm.

Chicken Squash Soup

Preparation time: 15 minutes
Cook time: 45 minutes
Nutrition facts (per serving): 270 Cal (16g fat, 16g protein, 5g fiber)

You won't know until you try it! That's what people told me about this soup, and it indeed tasted more unique and flavorsome than other chicken soups I've tried.

Ingredients (6 servings)
½ lb. boneless chicken thighs, cubed
1 onion, chopped
2 tablespoon olive oil
1 carrot, chopped
1 garlic clove, chopped
½ teaspoon mustard seeds, crushed
½ cup pearl barley
6 cups chicken broth
2 tablespoon parsley, minced
1 teaspoon fresh thyme leaves
1 small acorn squash, peeled, and diced
1 ½ cups broccoli florets
Salt and pepper

Preparation
Sauté onion, carrot, and garlic with oil in a deep skillet until soft. Stir in chicken and squash then sauté for 5 minutes. Add rest of the soup ingredients and cook for 30 minutes. Serve warm.

Alberta Soup

Preparation time: 15 minutes
Cook time: 60 minutes
Nutrition facts (per serving): 295 Cal (17g fat, 28g protein, 3g fiber)

If you haven't tried the Alberta soup before, then here comes a simple and easy cook this recipe that you can recreate at home in no time with minimum efforts.

Ingredients (6 servings)
4 large onions, thinly sliced
¼ cup butter
1 bottle light beer
5 cups beef broth
Salt and pepper

Topping
1 lb. tenderloin steaks or flank steak
2 tablespoon butter
4 eggs
8 slices baguette, toasted
1 tablespoon flat-leaf parsley, chopped

Preparation
Sauté the onion with the butter in a deep pan until soft. Add the steaks and cook for 3 minutes per side. Stir in the beer, broth, black pepper, and salt. Next, cook until the meat is tender. Beat the eggs and pour into the soup. Serve warm with parsley and baguette on top.

Newfoundland Dumpling Soup

Preparation time: 15 minutes
Cook time: 15 minutes
Nutrition facts (per serving): 312 Cal (10g fat, 21g protein, 4g fiber)

You can give this split pea dumpling soup a try because it has a good and delicious combination of split peas with carrots and dumplings.

Ingredients (6 servings)
1 cup yellow split peas
2 carrots, peeled and diced
1 leek, chopped
1 onion, chopped
½ rutabaga, peeled and diced
2 tablespoon olive oil
5 oz. salt pork, rind removed and diced
5 cups chicken broth
2 cups water
1 sprig fresh thyme
Salt and black pepper, to taste

Dumplings
½ cup all-purpose flour
½ teaspoon baking powder
1 pinch salt
2 tablespoon cold butter, diced
1 oz. grated sharp cheddar cheese
¼ cup milk

Preparation

Sauté the carrots, leek, onion, and rutabaga with oil in a deep pan for 5 minutes. Stir in the rest of the ingredients and cook until the split peas are soft. Meanwhile, mix the flour, baking powder, salt cold butter, cheese, and milk in a bowl. Divide the prepared dough into small dumplings and add them to the soup. Cook the soup for 5 minutes until soft. Serve warm.

Friend's Bean Soup

Preparation time: 15 minutes
Cook time: 40 minutes
Nutrition facts (per serving): 314 Cal (6g fat, 20g protein, 2g fiber)

This beans soup is loved by all, young and adult. Plus, it's quite simple and quick to make. This delight is great to serve at dinner tables.

Ingredients (4 servings)
2 tablespoon olive oil
3 garlic cloves, minced
1 medium onion, chopped
1 lb. turkey Italian sausages, casings removed
3 (15 ½ oz.) cans great Northern beans
2 (14.5 oz.) cans diced tomatoes
1 (14 oz.) can chicken broth
¾ teaspoon dried rosemary
Black pepper to taste

Preparation
Sauté the onion and the garlic with oil in a deep pan until soft. Stir in the sausages and sauté for 5 minutes. Stir in the rest of the ingredients, mix well, and cover to cook for 35 minutes on a simmer. Serve warm.

Hearty Tuscan Soup

Preparation time: 5 minutes
Cook time: 13 minutes
Nutrition facts (per serving): 204 Cal (9g fat, 6g protein, 1.7g fiber)

Try the hearty Tuscan soup at the dinner as the soup is infused with an amazing blend of veggies and spices. Serve warm with your favorite bread.

Ingredients (6 servings)
1 tablespoon olive oil
1 onion, chopped
1 garlic clove, minced
3 cups chicken broth
1 (14oz.) can navy beans
1 (14oz.) can dice tomatoes
2 cups packed kale, chopped
2 cups store-bought croutons
½ cup fresh basil, chopped
½ cup parmesan, grated

Preparation
Sauté the onion and garlic with oil in a deep skillet until soft. Stir in the broth, beans, and tomatoes and then cook for 5 minutes. Stir in the kale, basil, and Parmesan. Next, cook for 3 minutes. Spread the croutons in a baking sheet and roast for 5-mintues until golden brown. Add the croutons to the soup and serve warm.

Acorn Squash Soup with Warm Spices

Preparation time: 5 minutes
Cook time: 8 hours
Nutrition facts (per serving): 102 Cal (3g fat, 11g protein, 2g fiber)

This acorn squash soup is a typical Canadian entree, which is essential on the Canadian menu. It has this rich mix of acorn squash with cream that I love.

Ingredients (6 servings)
1 ½ lbs. acorn squash, diced
2 tablespoon vegetable oil
½ teaspoon salt
1 medium onion, chopped
2 garlic cloves, minced
½ teaspoon chili powder
½ teaspoon cumin
¼ teaspoon cinnamon
3 cups vegetable broth
1 cup water
¼ cup cream
1 tablespoon lime juice
½ cup pepitas
Sour cream, optional

Preparation

Add the chicken broth, tomatoes, and the rest of the ingredients to a slow cooker and cook for 8 hours on low heat. Discard the cloves and serve warm.

Cilantro-Lime Chicken Soup

Preparation time: 5 minutes
Cook time: 25 minutes
Nutrition facts (per serving): 320 Cal (32g fat, 13g protein, 0g fiber)

Simple and easy to make, this recipe is iconic on this menu. Canadian chicken soup is a delight for the dinner table.

Ingredients (4 servings)
1 tablespoon vegetable oil
1 6-inch tortilla, cut into bite sized strips
1 leek, thinly sliced
2 bell peppers, chopped
2 celery stalks, chopped
3 garlic cloves, minced
1 tablespoon dried oregano
¼ teaspoon hot-red-chili-flakes
¼ teaspoon nutmeg
1 cube chicken bouillon
2 boneless chicken breasts, sliced
1 cup frozen corn kernels
2 limes, juiced
½ cup cilantro, chopped

Preparation
Sauté the leek, bell peppers, celery, and chicken with oil in a deep pan for 10 minutes. Stir in the rest of the spices, 4 cups water and bouillon.

Cook for 10 minutes and then add the corn, lime juice, and cilantro. Cook for 5 minutes then garnish with tortilla strips. Serve.

Turkey and White-Bean Soup

Preparation time: 5 minutes
Cook time: 20 minutes
Nutrition facts (per serving): 365 Cal (32g fat, 29g protein, 2g fiber)

Turkey and white bean soup are one of the traditional Canadian entrées made from kidney beans, tomato paste, and kale.

Ingredients (6 servings)
1 lb. turkey sausages
1 small onion, diced
1 jalapeno, seeded and diced
1 garlic clove, minced
2 teaspoon chili powder
2 tablespoon tomato paste
4 cups chicken broth
2 cups canned white kidney beans, drained and rinsed
2 cups packed chopped kale
¼ cup lime juice

Preparation
Sauté the onion, garlic, and sausage in a deep skillet for 5 minutes. Stir in the rest of the ingredients and cook for 15 minutes on medium heat. Serve warm.

Classic Soup with Chicken and Shrimp

Preparation time: 5 minutes
Cook time: 4 hours
Nutrition facts (per serving): 116 Cal (3g fat, 11g protein, 0.8g fiber)

A perfect mix of chicken, shrimp and mushrooms in one soup is all that you need to expand your Canadian menu. Simple and easy to make, this recipe is a must to try.

Ingredients (6 servings)

4 cups chicken broth
2 cups from a can of regular coconut milk
½ teaspoon granulated sugar
1 teaspoon hot chili-garlic sauce
3 leaves kaffir lime
1 boneless chicken breast, cut into strips
½ lb. sliced mushrooms
1 ripe tomato, chopped
½ lb. medium shrimp, peeled
2 tablespoon lime juice
2 tablespoon fish sauce
¼ cup cilantro, chopped

Preparation

Add the chicken, milk, and the rest of the ingredients to a slow cooker, cover, and cook for 4 hours on low heat. Serve warm.

Canadian Yellow Split Pea Soup with Ham

Preparation time: 10 minutes
Cook time: 3 hours
Nutrition facts (per serving): 232 Cal (10g fat, 28g protein, 6g fiber)

This yellow soup with ham will melt your heart away with its epic flavors. This soup is filled with savory ham and carrot flavors.

Ingredients (4 servings)
2 ½ cups yellow split peas
1 ham bone with some meat
4 carrots, diced
½ large Spanish onion, diced
5 stalks celery, diced
2 teaspoon dried thyme
1 bay leaf
2 tablespoon salt
1 pinch black pepper, or to taste
8 cups water

Preparation
Add the split peas, ham bones, and the rest of the ingredients to a deep pan and cook to a boil. Reduce its heat, cover, and cook for 3 hours on low heat. Serve warm.

Mushroom Soup

Preparation time: 10 minutes
Cook time: 45 minutes
Nutrition facts (per serving): 201 Cal (14g fat, 9g protein, 3g fiber)

Let us have a rich and delicious combination of mushrooms with a creamy base in a soup. Try it with warm bread slices, and you will simply love it!

Ingredients (4 servings)
4 tablespoons unsalted butter
2 cups chopped onions
1-pound fresh mushrooms, sliced
2 teaspoons dried dill weed
1 tablespoon paprika
1 tablespoon soy sauce
2 cups chicken broth
1 cup milk
3 tablespoons all-purpose flour
1 teaspoon salt
Black pepper, to taste
2 teaspoons lemon juice
¼ cup chopped fresh parsley
½ cup sour cream

Preparation
Sauté the onions with butter in a cooking pot for 5 minutes. Stir in the mushrooms and sauté for 5 minutes. Add the paprika, soy sauce, dill,

and broth, and then cook for almost 15 minutes on a simmer. Mix the flour with milk in a small bowl. Pour this mixture into the soup and cook for almost 15 minutes with occasional stirring. Add the sour cream, parsley, lemon juice, black pepper, and salt. Mix and cook on low heat for 5 minutes. Serve warm.

Beefy Barley Soup

Preparation time: 15 minutes
Cook time: 45 minutes
Nutrition facts (per serving): 139 Cal (0g fat, 8g protein, 2g fiber)

Do you want to enjoy a barley soup with a Canadian twist? Then try this Canadian barley soup recipe. You can serve it with your favorite bread on the side.

Ingredients (6 servings)

1 tablespoon olive oil
1 onion, chopped
2 garlic cloves, minced
½ lb. cremini mushrooms, quartered
6 cups diced tomatoes, drained
½ cup pearl barley
2 bay leaves
2 teaspoon dried oregano leaves
6 cups beef broth
10 ½ oz. beef tenderloin grilling steak, cut into cubes
½ teaspoon salt

Preparation

Sauté the beef with oil in a deep skillet until brown. Stir in the mushrooms, onion, garlic, and tomatoes and then cook for 5 minutes. Add the rest of the ingredients and cook until the meat is tender. Serve warm.

Tomato Soup with Grilled Cheese Croutons

Preparation time: 15 minutes
Cook time: 35 minutes
Nutrition facts (per serving): 339 Cal (23g fat, 20g protein, 6g fiber)

The classic tomato soup with grilled crouton is here to complete your Canadian menu. This meal can be served on all special occasions and festive celebrations.

Ingredients (6 servings)
2 tablespoon butter
1 large onion, chopped
1 large garlic clove, minced
2 small carrots, peeled and chopped
2 small celery stalks, chopped
1 small, red bell pepper, chopped
2 tablespoon tomato paste
1 tablespoon lime juice
½ teaspoon granulated sugar
½ teaspoon salt
⅛ teaspoon cayenne pepper
3 cups chicken broth
27 oz. can dice tomatoes
2 tablespoon unsalted butter
4 slices white bread
2 square slices cheddar

Preparation

Sauté the onion, garlic, carrots, celery, and bell pepper with butter in a stock pot for 5 minutes. Stir in the tomatoes and the rest of the ingredients, except for the bread and the cheese. Cover and cook on a simmer for 20 minutes. Puree this soup with a blender. Place a grill pan on medium heat. Place a cheese slice on top of the two bread slices and place the other two slices on top. Grill the bread sandwich for 2 minutes per side. Cut the grilled cheese sandwiches into squares. Divide the soup into four cups and garnish with bread squares.

Canadian Vegetable Soup

Preparation time: 15 minutes
Cook time: 35 minutes
Nutrition facts (per serving): 570 Cal (46g fat, 12g protein, 2g fiber)

The Canadian vegetable soup is an entrée that you must serve at the winter dinner table. This recipe will add a lot of flavors, aromas, and colors to your menu.

Ingredients (6 servings)
2 quarts vegetable broth
⅔ cup celery, chopped
⅔ cup onion, chopped
1 garlic clove, chopped
½ cup carrots, sliced
1 cups potato, diced
1 tablespoon canola oil
¼ cup tomato paste
¼ cup green pepper, diced
¼ tablespoon sweet basil
Salt and black pepper to taste
¼ cup macaroni
¼ cup barley
1 cup chopped cabbage
½ tomato, chopped

Preparation

Sauté the onion, carrots, potatoes, garlic, and celery with oil in a deep skillet for 5 minutes. Stir in the rest of the ingredients, cover and cook on a simmer for 30 minutes. Serve warm.

Mushroom, Barley and Bacon Soup

Preparation time: 15 minutes
Cook time: 18 minutes
Nutrition facts (per serving): 138 Cal (6g fat, 4g protein, 1.2g fiber)

The Canadian mushroom barley soup is here to complete your Canadian menu. This meal can be served on all special occasions and memorable celebrations.

Ingredients (6 servings)
2 tablespoon butter
1 cup thinly sliced leeks
1 cup sliced carrots
4 cups prepackaged mushrooms, sliced
3 ½ quarts beef broth
½ cup quick cooking barley
1 cup milk
1 (6 oz.) package Canadian bacon, diced
1 tablespoon fresh thyme leaves, chopped
¼ teaspoon freshly black pepper

Preparation
Sauté the carrots and the leeks with the butter in a saucepan over medium heat for 2 minutes. Stir in the mushrooms and then sauté for 2 minutes. Add the black pepper, thyme, barley, and broth and then cook to a simmer. Cover and cook for 14 minutes on a simmer. Add the bacon and bacon and then serve with croutons and thyme on top. Serve warm.

Main Dishes

Montreal Smoked Meat

Preparation time: 10 minutes
Cook time: 2 hours
Nutrition facts (per serving): 231 Cal (9.5g fat, 9.7g protein, 9g fiber)

Who doesn't like Montreal smoked meat? Get ready to enjoy a heart-melting, smoked meat appetizer on this menu.

Ingredients (6 servings)
1 cup salt
3 tablespoon black pepper
3 tablespoon ground coriander
1 tablespoon pink salt
1 tablespoon sugar
1 teaspoon ground bay leaf
1 teaspoon ground cloves
1 whole (12-14 lbs.) brisket, fat trimmed

Rub
3 tablespoon black pepper
1 tablespoon ground coriander
1 tablespoon paprika
1 tablespoon garlic powder
1 tablespoon onion powder
1 teaspoon dill weed
1 teaspoon ground mustard
1 teaspoon celery seed
1 teaspoon crushed red pepper

Preparation

Mix the sugar, cloves, bay leaf, coriander, black pepper, salt, and pink salt in a small bowl. Add this prepared mixture and the brisket to a large Ziploc bag, seal the bag, and then refrigerate for 4 day for curing. Remove the brisket from the bag and soak it in water for 2 hours. Then drain and pat it dry. Mix the rest of the spices rub in a bowl and rub them over the brisket. Set a grill at 225 degrees F. Place the brisket in the grill, cover, and smoke for 6 hours almost, until the internal temperature reaches 165 degrees F. Transfer this brisket to a roasting and add the water up to 1 inch. Cover this pan with aluminum foil and roast for 2 hours. Slice and serve.

Glazed Cornish Hens with Pecan-Rice Stuffing

Preparation time: 10 minutes
Cook time: 1 hour 58 minutes
Nutrition facts (per serving): 550 Cal (17g fat, 5g protein, 1g fiber)

The Canadian Cornish hens are great to serve with all rice and salads on all the special occasions. This meal is perfect to serve during large gatherings.

Ingredients (8 servings)

8 (24 oz.) Cornish game hens
¼ cup butter, softened
½ teaspoon salt
½ teaspoon black pepper
2 cups unsweetened apple juice
1 tablespoon honey
1 tablespoon Dijon mustard

Pecan Rice

2 tablespoon butter
1-½ cups uncooked long grain rice
2 teaspoon ground cumin
1 teaspoon curry powder
4 cups chicken broth
1 cup chopped pecans, toasted
3 green onions, sliced
½ cup golden raisins

Preparation

Tuck the wings and tie the drumsticks. Mix the butter with black pepper and salt and then brush over the hens. Place the hens in a roasting pan and roast for 1 hour at 350 degrees F. Boil the apple juice in a small saucepan and cook until reduced to half. Add the mustard and the honey and then mix well. Brush this prepared mixture over the hens and bake for 35 minutes. Sauté the pecan rice with curry, cumin, and butter in a saucepan for 3 minutes. Add the broth and cook to a boil. Reduce the heat, cover, and cook for almost 20 minutes. Add the raisins, onions, and pecans. Spread this prepared mixture and the remaining apple glaze over the hens and serve.

Duo Tater Bake

Preparation time: 10 minutes
Cook time: 48 minutes
Nutrition facts (per serving): 236 Cal (12g g fat, 5g protein, 3g fiber)

The famous Canadian due tater bake! It's another special entrée on the Canadian menu. Try baking it at home with these healthy ingredients and enjoy it.

Ingredients (8 servings)
4 lbs. russet potatoes, peeled and cubed
3 lbs. sweet potatoes, peeled and cubed
2 cartons (8 oz.) chive and onion cream cheese
1 cup sour cream
¼ cup Colby-Monterey Jack cheese, shredded
⅓ cup milk
¼ cup Parmesan cheese, shredded
½ teaspoon salt
½ teaspoon black pepper

Topping
1 cup Colby-Monterey Jack cheese, shredded
½ cup green onions, chopped
¼ cup Parmesan cheese, shredded

Preparation
Add the russet potatoes and the water to a Dutch oven, cover, and cook for 15 minutes. Add the sweet potatoes and the water to a large

saucepan, cook to a boil, reduce the heat, cover, and cook for 15 minutes. Drain and mash the cooked sweet potatoes in a bowl. Stir in half of the cream cheese, sour cream, and Colby cheese and then mix well. Drain the russet potatoes, mash, and mix with the remaining sour cream, cream cheese, milk, black pepper, salt and Parmesan cheese in a bowl. Spread 2 ⅔ cup russet potato mixture in 2 greased 11x7 inch baking pans. Spread the 4 cups sweet potato mixture on top and repeat the layers. Bake the layers for 15 minutes at 350 degrees F. Mix the topping ingredients in a bowl and spread on top of the baked layers. Bake the cheese for 3 minutes. Serve warm.

Sticky Honey Chicken Wings

Preparation time: 10 minutes
Cook time: 25 minutes
Nutrition facts (per serving): 294 Cal (22g fat, 26g protein, 2g fiber)

Try the famous Canadian style chicken wings, which are seasoned with blossom honey and vinegar. Serve warm with fresh cucumber salad.

Ingredients (6 servings)
½ cup orange blossom honey
⅓ cup white vinegar
2 tablespoon paprika
2 teaspoon salt
1 teaspoon black pepper
4 lbs. chicken wings

Preparation
Toss the wings with honey, vinegar, salt, black pepper, and paprika in a bowl. Spread the wings on a baking sheet and then roast for 20-25 minutes. Serve warm.

Cranberry Maple Chicken

Preparation time: 10 minutes
Cook time: 25 minutes
Nutrition facts (per serving): 236 Cal (5g fat, 23g protein, 1g fiber)

You can serve this maple chicken with warm tortillas and the famous Canadian cob salad. Keep the cranberry sauce prepared for quick cooking.

Ingredients (6 servings)

2 cups fresh or frozen cranberries
¾ cup water
⅓ cup sugar
6 boneless chicken breasts halved
½ teaspoon salt
¼ teaspoon black pepper
1 tablespoon canola oil
¼ cup maple syrup

Preparation

Combine the sugar, water and cranberries in a small saucepan over medium heat and cook for 15 minutes. Mix the chicken with the black pepper and the salt. Sear the chicken and cook for 5 minutes per side. Add the cranberry on top and serve warm.

Caribou Canadian Stew

Preparation time: 10 minutes
Cook time: 2 hours 20 minutes
Nutrition facts (per serving): 481 Cal (16g fat, 29g protein, 2g fiber)

The traditional Canadian caribou stew is here to add flavors to your dinner table, but this time with a mix of lamb and potatoes. You can try it as an effortless entrée with all sorts of bread.

Ingredients (6 servings)
2 tablespoon vegetable oil
1 lb. lamb cutlets
2 lbs. potatoes, peeled and quartered
1 cup chopped carrots
1 cup chopped onion
1 cup sliced leeks, cleaned
2 tablespoon all-purpose flour
3 cups dark beef stock
3 cabbage leaves, sliced
Salt, to taste
Black pepper, to taste

Preparation
At 350 degrees F, preheat your oven. Sauté the lamb piece with 1 tablespoon oil in a cooking pot until brown. Transfer the brown meat to a Dutch oven. Top the lamb with the potatoes, carrots, onion, and leeks. Add the flour to the lamb drippings in the cooking pot and then sauté for 3 minutes. Stir in 1 cup stock, mix, and cook until the mixture

thickens. Pour this sauce over the lamb and the veggies. Add the remaining stock and cook for 1 hour. Stir in the cabbage, uncover, and cook for 1 hour. Serve warm.

Canadian Beef Stew

Preparation time: 10 minutes
Cook time: 85 minutes
Nutrition facts (per serving): 401 Cal (14g fat, 29g protein, 3g fiber)

Let's have a rich and delicious combination of beef with veggies. Try it with warm bread slices, and you'll simply love it.

Ingredients (6 servings)
1 ¼ lb. chuck beef stew meat, cut into chunks
3 teaspoon of salt
¼ cup olive oil
6 large garlic cloves, minced
4 cups beef stock
2 cups water
1 cup of Guinness stout
1 cup of red wine
2 tablespoon tomato paste
1 tablespoon sugar
1 tablespoon dried thyme
1 tablespoon Worcestershire sauce
2 bay leaves
2 tablespoon butter
3 lbs. russet potatoes, peeled, cut into pieces
1 large onion, chopped
2 cups peeled carrots, chopped
½ teaspoon black pepper
2 tablespoon fresh parsley, chopped

Preparation

Sauté the beef pieces with oil in a suitable cooking pot until brown. Stir in the garlic and then sauté for 30 seconds. Stir in the bay leaves, Worcestershire sauce, thyme, sugar, tomato paste, red wine, Guinness, water, and stock and then mix well. Cook the mixture on low heat and cook for 1 hour. Sauté the onions and the carrots with butter in a separate skillet for 15 minutes. Add these veggies to the stew and adjust the seasoning with the black pepper and the salt. Finally, cook for 40 minutes. Discard the bay leaves. Garnish with parsley. Serve warm.

Hodge Podge

Preparation time: 15 minutes
Cook time: 20 minutes
Nutrition facts (per serving): 365 Cal (17g fat, 25g protein, 5.4g fiber)

It's about time to try some classic Hodge podge stew on the menu and make it more diverse and flavorsome. Serve warm with your favorite herbs on top.

Ingredients (6 servings)
4 cups fresh vegetables
2 tablespoon unsalted butter
3 cups cream
1 cup water
2 tablespoon cornstarch
¼ cup chopped fresh herbs
Salt and black pepper, to taste

Preparation
Sauté the butter with vegetables in a deep pan for 5 minutes. Mix the cornstarch with a beater in a small bowl. Add the cream, cornstarch mixture, and water to the veggies and cook on low heat for 15 minutes. Add the black pepper and the salt to the Hodge podge. Garnish with dill and chives. Serve warm.

Chunky Creamy Chicken Stew

Preparation time: 15 minutes
Cook time: 4 hours 30 minutes
Nutrition facts (per serving): 229 Cal (7g fat, 24g protein, 0.6g fiber)

Canadian creamy chicken stew is great to complete your menu; and this one, in particular, is excellent for a nutritious diet.

Ingredients (6 servings)
1 ½ lbs. boneless chicken breasts, cut into strips
2 teaspoon canola oil
⅔ cup onion, chopped
2 medium carrots, chopped
2 celery ribs, chopped
1 cup frozen corn
2 cans (10-¾ oz.) condensed cream of potato soup, undiluted
1-½ cups chicken broth
1 teaspoon dill weed
1 cup frozen peas
½ cup half-and-half cream

Preparation
Sauté the chicken with oil in a deep skillet until brown. Transfer it to a slow cooker. Add the corn, celery, carrots, and onion. Blend the soup with the broth in a bowl and add to the slow cooker. Cover and cook on low heat for 4 hours. Add the cream and the peas, cover, and cook for 30 minutes. Serve warm.

Cauliflower Stew

Preparation time: 15 minutes
Cook time: 17 minutes
Nutrition facts (per serving): 338 Cal (10g fat, 33g protein, 3g fiber)

Now you can quickly make a flavorsome Canadian cauliflower stew at home and serve it to have a fancy meal for yourself and your guest.

Ingredients (6 servings)
1 head cauliflower, florets
1 carrot, shredded
¼ cup celery, chopped
2 ½ cups water
2 teaspoon chicken bouillon
3 tablespoon butter
3 tablespoon all-purpose flour
¾ teaspoon salt
⅛ teaspoon black pepper
2 cups milk
1 cup cheddar cheese, shredded
1 teaspoon hot pepper sauce

Preparation
Boil the water, celery, carrot, cauliflower, and bouillon in a Dutch oven. Reduce the heat, cover, and cook for 15 minutes on a simmer. Mix the flour with the black pepper, salt, and milk in a skillet and cook for 2 minutes with continuous stirring until the mixture thickens. Add the cheese and cook until the mixture is melted. Add this sauce and the hot pepper sauce to the cauliflower. Mix well and serve warm.

Turkey Tetrazzini

Preparation time: 10 minutes
Cook time: 30 minutes
Nutrition facts (per serving): 378 Cal (11g fat, 25g protein, 3g fiber)

If you haven't tried the turkey tetrazzini before, then here comes a simple and easy to cook recipe that you can recreate at home in no time with minimum efforts.

Ingredients (6 servings)

1 package (7 oz.) thin spaghetti, broken in half
2 cups cubed cooked turkey
1 cup sliced fresh mushrooms
1 small onion, chopped
3 tablespoon butter
1 can (10-¾ oz.) condensed cream of mushroom soup
1 cup milk
½ teaspoon poultry seasoning
⅛ teaspoon ground mustard
1 cup shredded cheddar cheese
1 cup shredded part-skim mozzarella cheese
1 tablespoon shredded Parmesan cheese
Minced fresh parsley, to taste

Preparation

Cook the spaghetti as per the cooking directions and then drain. Spread the spaghetti in an 11x7 inch baking dish and top them with turkey. Sauté the onion, mushrooms, and butter in a deep skillet until soft. Stir in the milk, poultry seasoning, mustard, soup, and cheese; then cook until the cheese is melted. Pour this prepared mixture over the turkey. Drizzle the remaining cheese on top and bake for 30 minutes at 350 degrees F. Garnish with parsley. Serve warm.

Sweet Potato Stuffing

Preparation time: 10 minutes
Cook time: 4 hours
Nutrition facts (per serving): 212 Cal (8g fat, 5g protein, 2g fiber)

Try making this delicious potato stuffing with a unique combination of butter, onion, and sweet potatoes at home to enjoy the best of the Canadian flavors.

Ingredients (6 servings)

¼ cup butter, cubed
½ cup chopped celery
½ cup chopped onion
½ cup chicken broth
½ teaspoon salt
½ teaspoon poultry seasoning
½ teaspoon rubbed sage
½ teaspoon pepper
6 cups dry bread cubes
1 large sweet potato, cooked, peeled and cubed
¼ cup chopped pecans

Preparation

Sauté the onion, celery, and butter in a 6 qt slow cooker until soft. Stir in the seasonings, broth, and the rest of the ingredients. Cover and cook for almost 4 hours on low heat. Serve warm.

Scalloped Potatoes

Preparation time: 10 minutes
Cook time: 67 minutes
Nutrition facts (per serving): 396 Cal (13g fat, 22g protein, 4g fiber)

This loaded scalloped potatoes meal brings all the delicious Canadian delights in one place, including potatoes, cheese, and milk.

Ingredients (6 servings)
2 tablespoon butter
3 tablespoon all-purpose flour
1 teaspoon salt
¼ teaspoon pepper
1-½ cups fat-free milk
½ cup Kerry gold Dubliner Aged Cheese
2 lbs. red potatoes, peeled and thinly sliced
1 cup onions, sliced

Preparation
At 350 degrees F, preheat your oven. Sauté the flour, black pepper, and salt with the butter in a small saucepan until smooth. Stir in the milk and cook to a boil. Mix and cook the mixture for 2 minutes until it thickens. Remove the mixture from the heat and add the cheese. Grease an suitable 8-inch baking dish with cooking spray. Spread half of the potatoes in this dish and top them with ½ cup onion and half of the cheese sauce. Repeat the layers and cover to bake for 50 minutes. Uncover and bake for another 15 minutes. Serve warm.

Pastry-Topped Turkey Casserole

Preparation time: 10 minutes
Cook time: 42 minutes
Nutrition facts (per serving): 280 Cal (4g fat, 23g protein, 0.5g fiber)

This turkey casserole makes a flavorsome serving with bread, so pair it with your dinner or as a good delicious lunch on your table.

Ingredients (6 servings)
2 cups diced red potatoes
1 large onion, chopped
2 celery ribs, chopped
2 teaspoon chicken bouillon granules
½ teaspoon dried rosemary, crushed
¼ teaspoon garlic powder
¼ teaspoon dried thyme
⅛ teaspoon pepper
1 can (14-½ oz.) chicken broth
3 cups mixed vegetables
½ cup water
3 tablespoon all-purpose flour
⅔ cup evaporated milk
2 cups cubed cooked turkey breast

Crust
¼ cup all-purpose flour
¼ cup whole wheat flour
½ teaspoon baking powder
⅛ teaspoon salt
4 tablespoon fat-free milk
1 tablespoon canola oil
1 paprika

Preparation

At 400 degrees F, preheat your oven. Boil the potatoes, onion, celery, bouillon, rosemary, garlic powder, thyme, black pepper, broth, milk, vegetables, and turkey in a cooking pan. Next, cover and cook on a simmer for 15 minutes. Mix the flour with the milk in a bowl, pour into the turkey mixture, and cook for 2 minutes until the mixture thickens. Spread this turkey mixture in an 8-inch square baking dish. Mix the crust ingredients in a bowl to make dough. Roll the prepared dough into ⅛-inch-thick sheet and cut into strips. Arrange the strips over the filling and brush them with milk. Drizzle the paprika on top. Bake the casserole for 25 minutes in the oven. Slice and serve.

Baked Chicken Schnitzel

Preparation time: 10 minutes
Cook time: 12 minutes
Nutrition facts (per serving): 260 Cal (13g fat, 17g protein, 4g fiber)

Let's make a chicken schnitzel with these simple ingredients. Mix them together and then cook to have great flavors.

Ingredients (6 servings)

1 tablespoon olive oil, or as desired
6 chicken breasts, cut in half lengthwise
salt and black pepper to taste
¾ cup all-purpose flour
1 tablespoon paprika
2 eggs, beaten
2 cups seasoned bread crumbs
1 large lemon, zested

Preparation

At 425 degrees F, preheat your oven. Layer a large baking sheet with foil sheet and grease with oil. Flatten the chicken into ¼ inch thickness and season them with black pepper and salt. Mix the flour with the paprika in a bowl. Beat the eggs with the black pepper and the salt in a shallow bowl. Mix the breadcrumbs with the lemon zest on a large plate. Coat the prepared chicken with the flour mixture and dip in the egg and coat with the breadcrumb's mixture. Place the coated chicken onto the baking sheet. Drizzle olive oil on top and bake for 6 minutes. Flip the chicken and bake for 6 minutes. Serve warm.

Greek Lemon Chicken and Potato Bake

Preparation time: 10 minutes
Cook time: 60 minutes
Nutrition facts (per serving): 394 Cal (19 g fat, 13g protein, 1g fiber)

Count on this potato chicken bake to make your dinner extra special and surprise your loved one with the ultimate flavors.

Ingredients (4 servings)
4 chicken leg quarters
1 (24 oz.) bag small potatoes
½ cup olive oil
2 lemons, juiced
2 tablespoon dried basil
2 tablespoon dried oregano
1 tablespoon salt
1 tablespoon black pepper
2 tablespoon lemon and herb seasoning
1 (12 oz.) package fresh green beans

Preparation
At 425 degrees F, preheat your oven. Grease a suitable large baking sheet with cooking oil. Spread the chicken quarters on the prepared baking sheet. Toss the potatoes with the lemon seasoning, black pepper, salt, oregano, basil, lemon juice, and olive oil in a bowl. Spread the potatoes around the chicken with the remaining oil and the lemon juice on top. Bake the chicken for 30 minutes. Shake the potatoes and bake for 15 minutes. Spread the green beans around the chicken. Bake again for 15 minutes. Serve warm.

Danielle's Seafood Chowder

Preparation time: 10 minutes
Cook time: 24 minutes
Nutrition facts (per serving): 291 Cal (33g fat, 9g protein, 2g fiber)

This seafood chowder is known as the classic Canadian entrees. With corn, potatoes, and lobster meat used, this chowder is super rich and nutritious.

Ingredients (6 servings)

⅓ cup butter
1 teaspoon olive oil
1 onion, minced
⅓ cup all-purpose flour
1 quart half-and-half
2 cups clams, with juice reserved
⅓ cup Parmigiano-Reggiano cheese, grated
2 potatoes, peeled and diced
2 cups cream-style corn
1 large ear corn, kernels cut from the cob
1 fresh haddock fillet, diced
2 cups large shrimp, peeled and deveined
1 cup sliced cherry tomatoes
1½ cups water
Salt and black pepper to taste
1 cup canned lobster meat, with juice

Preparation

Sauté the onion with the olive oil and the butter in a large pot over medium-low heat for 5 minutes. Stir in the flour, clam juice, half and half, cheese, and the onion mixture and then cook for 2 minutes. Stir in the cherry tomatoes, corn kernels, corn, and potatoes. Pour ½ cup water on top and cook on a simmer for 15 minutes. Add the black pepper, salt, shrimp, haddock, and drained clams and then cook for 2 minutes. Add the lobster and its juice. Serve warm.

Salmon and Potato Pie

Preparation time: 5 minutes
Cook time: 60 minutes
Nutrition facts (per serving): 413 Cal (18g fat, 10g protein, 6g fiber)

Canadian salmon and potato pie represents one of the most delicious entrée meals to try. You can add different variations for its toppings as well.

Ingredients (8 servings)
6 potatoes, peeled
1 small onion, minced
1 garlic clove, minced
1 tablespoon butter
1 (6 oz.) can red salmon, undrained
1 teaspoon dried thyme
1 cup milk
2 (9 inch) unbaked pie shells
1 to taste salt and pepper

Preparation
At 400 degrees F, preheat your oven. Boil 6 peeled potatoes in salted water for 15 minutes and then drain. Chop the potatoes and keep them aside. Sauté the garlic, onions, and butter in a skillet over medium heat until soft. Stir in the cooked potatoes and salmon and then mash the mixture. Spread a pie shell on a pie plate and spread the potato mixture on top. Spread the second pie shell on top. Cut small slits on top and bake for 45 minutes. Slice and serve warm.

Best Fried Walleye

Preparation time: 10 minutes
Cook time: 6 minutes
Nutrition facts (per serving): 281 Cal (14g fat, 22g protein, 1g fiber)

If you haven't tried the Canadian fried walleye before, then here comes a simple and easy to cook recipe that you can recreate at home in no time with minimum efforts.

Ingredients (4 servings)
4 walleye fillets
2 eggs, beaten
½ cup all-purpose flour
½ teaspoon garlic powder
1 pinch salt
½ teaspoon black pepper
2 cups crushed saltine crackers
Vegetable oil for frying
1 lemon, cut into wedges

Preparation
Cut the fillets into small sizes. Beat the eggs in a bowl and mix the flour with the black pepper, salt and garlic powder in a plate. Spread the breadcrumbs in a bowl. Set a deep-frying pan with oil and heat to 375 degrees F. Coat the chicken with the flour mixture, dip them in the eggs, and coat with the breadcrumbs. Deep fry the fillets for 3 minutes per side. Serve.

Sautéed Fiddleheads

Preparation time: 10 minutes
Cook time: 20 minutes
Nutrition facts (per serving): 390 Cal (23g fat, 28g protein, 6 g fiber)

This sautéed fiddlehead recipe is one of a kind and it has unique flavors due to its mix of fiddleheads with garlic and lemon juice. Serve warm with rice or bread.

Ingredients (6 servings)
3 cups fresh fiddlehead ferns, ends trimmed
3 tablespoon olive oil
1 garlic clove, minced
½ teaspoon sea salt
½ teaspoon black pepper
1 tablespoon fresh lemon juice

Preparation
Boil the salted water in a suitable pot and add the fiddlehead ferns. Cook the ferns for 10 minutes and then drain. Sauté the prepared fiddlehead ferns, black pepper, salt, and garlic with olive oil in a large skillet for 5 minutes. Stir in the lemon juice and mix well. Serve warm.

Real Poutine

Preparation time: 10 minutes
Cook time: 15 minutes
Nutrition facts (per serving): 441 Cal (21g fat, 33g protein, 3g fiber)

Best to serve at dinner, this real poutine can be served as an energizing meal. Here's a Canadian version of delicious fries.

Ingredients (6 servings)
1-quart vegetable oil for frying
1 (10.25 oz.) can beef gravy
5 medium potatoes, cut into fries
2 cups cheese curds

Preparation
Add the vegetable oil to a suitable deep pan and heat to 365 degrees F. Add the potatoes fries to the oil and cook until golden brown. Transfer all the fries to a plate and top with the beef gravy and the cheese curd. Serve.

Holiday Tourtiere

Preparation time: 10 minutes
Cook time: 1 hour 25 minutes
Nutrition facts (per serving): 379 Cal (11g fat, 4g protein, 3g fiber)

If you haven't tried this dish before, then here comes a memorable one.

Ingredients (6 servings)
2 ½ cups all-purpose flour
½ teaspoon salt
¾ cup cold lard, cubed
¼ cup cold unsalted butter, cubed
¼ cup ice water

Filling
2 tablespoon canola oil
4 slices bacon, chopped
6 garlic cloves, minced
1 large onion, chopped
2 teaspoon dried leaves of summer savory
1 ½ teaspoon salt
1 teaspoon celery salt
¾ teaspoon black pepper
½ teaspoon ground cloves
½ teaspoon ground nutmeg
1 lb. medium ground beef
½ lb. medium ground pork
½ cup russet potato, peeled and grated
½ cup beef broth
1 cup parsley, chopped
2 tablespoon maple syrup

Egg wash
1 egg yolk with 1 teaspoon water

Preparation
Blend the lard, flour, and salt in a food processor until crumbly. Add the ice water and mix until it makes smooth dough. Divide the prepared dough in half and wrap the prepared dough into a log. Refrigerate the prepared dough for 1 hour. Sauté the garlic, bacon, spices, and onion in a skillet for 5 minutes. Add the beef, pork, potato, and broth and then cook for 15 minutes. Mash the meat a little and add the parsley and the maple syrup. Cook for 5 minutes and then spread this prepared mixture in a baking sheet. At 400 degrees F, preheat your oven. Roll the prepared dough on a working surface onto a ¼ inch thick sheet. Spread one dough half into a 9-inch pie plate and refrigerate for 20 minutes. Roll the remaining dough into a ¼ inch thick sheet. Spread the prepared pie filling in the prepared dough and cover with the remaining dough on top. Brush the prepared dough with egg wash and bake for 60 minutes in the oven. Serve warm.

Oven-Fried Potatoes

Preparation time: 15 minutes
Cook time: 50 minutes
Nutrition facts (per serving): 250 Cal (6g fat, 12g protein, 10g fiber)

The famous over fried potatoes are essential to try on this Canadian menu. Bake them at home with these healthy ingredients and enjoy them.

Ingredients (6 servings)

12 medium potatoes, peeled and cubed

¼ cup Parmesan cheese, grated

2 teaspoon salt

1 teaspoon garlic powder

1 teaspoon paprika

½ teaspoon black pepper

⅓ cup vegetable oil

Preparation

Toss the potatoes with Parmesan cheese and seasonings in a bowl. Spread the potatoes in two baking pan and bake for 50 minutes at 375 degrees F. Serve warm.

Crispy Ginger Beef

Preparation time: 15 minutes
Cook time: 12 minutes
Nutrition facts (per serving): 419 Cal (14g fat, 19g protein, 7g fiber)

Gingered beef is one option to go for in dinner. Sure, it takes some time to get it ready, but it's a great taste worth all the time and effort.

Ingredients (4 servings)

¾ cup cornstarch
½ cup water
2 eggs
1-pound flank steak, cut into strips
½ cup canola oil
1 large carrot, cut into sticks
1 green bell pepper, cut into sticks
1 red bell pepper, cut into sticks
3 green onions, chopped
¼ cup fresh ginger root, minced
5 garlic cloves, minced
½ cup white sugar
¼ cup rice vinegar
3 tablespoon soy sauce
1 tablespoon sesame oil
1 tablespoon red pepper flakes

Preparation

Mix the cornstarch with the water in a bowl. Beat the eggs with the cornstarch mixture in a bowl. Dip the beef strips in this prepared mixture to coat. Add the oil to a cooking pan and heat it to 350 degrees F. Fry the beef strips for 3 minutes per side and then transfer to a plate. Add 1 tablespoon oil and veggies to a deep skillet and sauté for 3 minutes. Mix the red pepper, oil, soy sauce, rice vinegar, and sugar in a small bowl. Pour this prepared mixture over the vegetables and cook the mixture to a boil. Add the fried beef and cook for 3 minutes. Serve warm.

Canadian Tourtiere

Preparation time: 5 minutes
Cook time: 45 minutes
Nutrition facts (per serving): 376 Cal (14g fat, 22g protein, 18g fiber)

This Canadian Tourtiere recipe will make your day with a delightful taste. Serve warm with your favorite salad on the side.

Ingredients (6 servings)
1-pound lean ground pork
½ pound lean ground beef
1 onion, diced
1 garlic clove, minced
½ cup water
1 ½ teaspoon salt
½ teaspoon dried thyme, crushed
¼ teaspoon ground sage
¼ teaspoon black pepper
⅛ teaspoon ground cloves
1 recipe pastry for a 9-inch double crust pie

Preparation
Mix the pork, cloves, black pepper, sage, thyme, salt, water, garlic, beef, and onion in a saucepan, cover, and cook to a boil. Reduce the heat and cook on a simmer for 5 minutes. At 425 degrees F, preheat your oven. Spread the pie crust in a pie plate and top them with the meat mixture. Place the remaining pie crust on top and cut the small slits on top. Cover

the pie edges with a foil sheet and bake for 20 minutes in the oven. Remove the foil from top and bake again for 20 minutes. Allow the pie to cool and serve.

Canadian Pork Loin Chops

Preparation time: 15 minutes
Cook time: 17 minutes
Nutrition facts (per serving): 349 Cal (7g fat, 29g protein, 3g fiber)

If you want some new flavors in your meals, then this pork loin chops recipe is best to bring variety to the menu.

Ingredients (6 servings)
Spice Rub
1 ½ tablespoon brown sugar
1 ½ teaspoon sea salt
½ teaspoon garlic powder
½ teaspoon onion powder
½ teaspoon paprika
¼ teaspoon freshly black pepper
¼ teaspoon dry mustard
¼ teaspoon fennel seeds, crushed
6 pork loin chops, boneless, ½ inch thick

Glaze
¼ cup maple syrup
2 tablespoon spicy brown mustard
1 pinch garlic powder
1 pinch paprika
1 pinch black pepper
1 pinch cayenne pepper
½ cup seasoned bread crumbs

1 tablespoon olive oil

1 tablespoon canola oil

1 clove garlic clove, crushed

Preparation

Mix all the pork spice rub ingredients in a bowl and rub over the pork loin chops. Cover and marinate the chops for 6 hours. Mix the breadcrumbs with the oil and the garlic in a bowl. Coat the pork loin with the breadcrumbs and sear for 6 minutes per side in a greased skillet. Pour the glaze over the pork loin. Cook for 5 minutes on a simmer and serve.

Christmas Brunch Casserole

Preparation time: 5 minutes
Cook time: 1 hour 5 minutes
Nutrition facts (per serving): 543 Cal (26g fat, 22g protein, 0.3g fiber)

Here's a special Canadian brunch casserole, which is great to serve at special dinners and celebrations. Enjoy this casserole with mixed vegetable salad on the side.

Ingredients (6 servings)
11 lbs. bacon
2 onions, chopped
2 cups fresh sliced mushrooms
1 tablespoon butter
4 cups frozen hash brown potatoes, thawed
1 teaspoon salt
¼ teaspoon salt
½ teaspoon black pepper
4 eggs
1 ½ cups milk
1 pinch dried parsley
1 cup Cheddar cheese, shredded

Preparation
Sauté the bacon in a large skillet until crispy and transfer to a plate. Crumble the crispy bacon. Add the onion and the mushrooms to the skillet then sauté for 5 minutes. Grease a 9x13 inch casserole dish with

butter. Spread the potatoes in the dish and drizzle black pepper, garlic salt and salt on top. Add the onion and the mushrooms mixture and bacon on top. Beat the eggs with parsley and milk in a bowl Pour this prepared mixture over the potatoes and drizzle the cheese on top. Cover and refrigerate overnight. At 400 degrees F, preheat your oven. Bake the casserole for 1 hour. Slice and serve warm.

Desserts

Filled Strawberries

Preparation time: 10 minutes

Nutrition facts (per serving): 41 Cal (3g fat, 1g protein, 1.4g fiber)

Cream cheese Filled strawberries are here to make your meal special. In desserts, they give you a delicious and healthy combination of ingredients.

Ingredients (6 servings)

3 dozen large fresh strawberries

11 oz. cream cheese, softened

½ cup confectioners' sugar

¼ teaspoon almond extract

Grated chocolate, optional

Preparation

Cut an large X on the tip of each strawberry. Mix the cream cheese with sugar and almond extract in a bowl. Divide the cream cheese mixture in the strawberries and garnish with chocolate. Serve.

Canadian Cinnamon Rolls

Preparation time: 15 minutes
Cook time: 30 minutes
Nutrition facts (per serving): 456 Cal (15g fat, 6g protein, 0.7g fiber)

If you haven't tried these cinnamon rolls, then here comes a simple and easy to cook recipe that you can recreate at home in no time with minimum efforts.

Ingredients (6 servings)
1 cup milk
1 egg, beaten
4 tablespoon melted butter
4 tablespoon water
½ (3.5 oz.) package vanilla pudding mix
4 cups bread flour
1 tablespoon white sugar
½ teaspoon salt
2 ¼ teaspoon bread machine yeast
½ cup butter, softened
1 cup packed brown sugar
2 teaspoon ground cinnamon
¼ cup chopped walnuts
¼ cup raisins
1 teaspoon milk
1 ½ cups confectioners' sugar
4 tablespoon butter, softened
1 teaspoon vanilla extract

Preparation

Blend the milk with the yeast, salt, sugar, bread flour, vanilla pudding mix, water, melted butter, and egg in a bread machine. Knead the prepared dough for 5 minutes. Mix the brown sugar, 2 tsp cinnamon and butter in a bowl. Roll the prepared dough into a rectangle and drizzle the cinnamon mixture over the prepared dough. Top this prepared mixture over the raisins and walnuts. Roll the prepared dough into a log and pinch the seams. Cut the roll into thick slices. Place the cinnamon rolls in a greased 9x13 inch baking pan. Cover and leave the rolls for 10 minutes. At 350 degrees F, preheat your oven. Bake the cinnamon rolls for 20 minutes. Mix 4 tablespoon butter, sugar, milk, and vanilla in a small bowl. Pour this prepared mixture over the cinnamon rolls. Serve.

Caramel Fudge Cheesecake

Preparation time: 15 minutes
Cook time: 60 minutes
Nutrition facts (per serving): 635 Cal (38g fat, 10g protein, 2g fiber)

This new version of Canadian caramel fudge cheesecake is amazing, and it's simple and easy to cook. It's great for all the fudge lovers.

Ingredients (6 servings)
1 package fudge brownie mix
1 package (14 oz.) caramels
¼ cup evaporated milk
1 ¼ cups pecans, chopped
2 packages (8 oz. each) cream cheese
½ cup sugar
2 large eggs, beaten
2 oz. unsweetened chocolate, melted

Preparation
Prepare the brownie mix as per the package's direction. Grease a 9-inch springform pan with baking paper. Spread the prepared brownie batter in the pan and bake for 20 minutes at 350 degrees F. Allow the baked cake to cool for 10 minutes. Mix the melted caramels with milk in a bowl and pour over the brownie crust and drizzle the pecans on top. Beat the cream cheese with sugar and eggs in a mixing bowl on low speed. Stir in the melted chocolate and then mix well. Spread this prepared mixture over the pecans. Bake again for 40 minutes and then allow it to cool for 10 minutes. Serve.

Peanut Butter Graham Bars

Preparation time: 15 minutes
Cook time: 3 minutes
Nutrition facts (per serving): 187 Cal (9g fat, 2g protein, 1g fiber)

These peanut butter bars are always an easy way to add extra flavors and essential nutrients to your menu. Accordingly, here are some that you can make in just a few minutes.

Ingredients (8 servings)

10 whole graham crackers, broken
1 cup graham cracker crumbs
¾ cup sugar
½ cup packed brown sugar
½ cup butter, cubed
⅓ cup whole milk
½ cup semisweet chocolate chips
¼ cup creamy peanut butter

Preparation

Layer an 11x7 inch baking dish with half of the graham crackers. Mix the remaining crumbs with milk, butter, and sugars in a bowl and heat in the microwave for 2 minutes. Mix well, spread over the cracker crust, and then add the remaining graham crackers on top. Spread the rest of the sugar mixture over the cracker layer. Melt the chocolate chips with the peanut butter in a bowl by heating in the microwave for 45 seconds until melted. Mix well and pour over the bars. Cover and refrigerate the bars for 2 hours then cut into squares. Serve.

Old-Fashioned Buttermilk Biscuits

Preparation time: 15 minutes
Cook time: 12 minutes
Nutrition facts (per serving): 142 Cal (4g fat, 4g protein, 3g fiber)

Here's a delicious and savory combination of butter milk, flour, and sour cream that you must add to your menu.

Ingredients (6 servings)
1-¾ cups all-purpose flour
2 teaspoon baking powder
½ teaspoon baking soda
½ teaspoon sugar
¼ teaspoon salt
⅔ cup buttermilk
2 tablespoon canola oil
1 tablespoon sour cream

Preparations
Mix the salt, sugar, baking soda, baking powder, and flour in a bowl. Stir in the sour cream, oil, and buttermilk then mix well. Knead this prepared dough for 10 minutes. Roll out the prepared dough into ½ inch thick and cut 2 ½ inch rounds using a cookie cutter. Place each cookie round in a greased baking sheet and bake for 12 minutes at 400 degrees F. Serve.

Cranberry Butter Crunch Bark

Preparation time: 15 minutes
Cook time: 2 minutes
Nutrition facts (per serving): 336 Cal (18g fat, 0g protein, 1.7g fiber)

A perfect mix of white candy and cranberry inside is worth trying. Serve with your favorite drink and toasted nuts.

Ingredients (6 servings)
1 cup and ½ teaspoon butter
1 cup sugar
3 tablespoon water
8 cups white candy coating, chopped
3 cups dried cranberries

Preparation
Grease a 15x10 inch baking pan with ½ teaspoon of butter. Melt 1 cup butter in a saucepan over medium low heat. Add the water and the sugar and cook until the temperature reaches 290 degrees F. Spread the toffee mixture in a suitable baking sheet lined with parchment paper and refrigerate for 1 hour until hard. Break the toffee into small pieces. Next, chop the toffee in a food processor. Grease two 15x10 inch baking pans with butter. Melt 4 cups white candy coating in a bowl by heating in the microwave. Stir in the dried cranberries and half of the toffee pieces and mix evenly. Spread this prepared mixture in one prepared pan. Repeat the same steps with the remaining ingredients and spread this prepared mixture in another prepared pan. Refrigerate the candy mixtures and break into pieces. Serve.

Chocolate Peanut Butter Candy

Preparation time: 15 minutes
Cook time: 2 minutes
Nutrition facts (per serving): 316 Cal (21g fat, 5g protein, 0g fiber)

Are you in a mood to have some candy on the menu? Well, you can serve these delicious peanut butter candies using this simple recipe.

Ingredients (8 servings)
1 lb. white candy coating, chopped
1-½ cups creamy peanut butter
2 cups semisweet chocolate chips

Preparation
Melt the white candy coating in a bowl by heating in the microwave. Sir in the peanut butter and mix well. Spread this prepared mixture in a baking sheet lined with baking paper. Melt the chocolate chips in a bowl by heating in the microwave. Drizzle the chocolate over the candy and make swirls. Refrigerate the candy for 1 hour. Break the candy into pieces. Serve.

Mint Angel Cake

Preparation time: 10 minutes
Cook time: 50 minutes
Nutrition facts (per serving): 213 Cal (10g fat, 4g protein, 5g fiber)

Canadian angel cake is one delicious way to complete your Canadian dessert menu. In turn, here's a recipe that you can try for a lovely treat.

Ingredients (8 servings)
12 large egg whites
1 cup cake flour
1 teaspoon cream of tartar
1 teaspoon almond extract
¼ teaspoon salt
1-¼ cups sugar
¼ cup 3 tablespoon crushed peppermint candies
¼ cup water
1 ¾ cups heavy whipping cream

Preparation
At 350 degrees F, preheat your oven. Beat the 12 egg whites with cream of tartar, salt, and almond extract in a bowl until foamy. Stir in the sugar and continue beating until they form stiff peaks. Add the flour and mix evenly. Spread this batter in a 10-inch tube pan and bake for 50 minutes. Flip the cake on a plate and allow it to cool. Mix ¼ cup of crushed candies and water in a saucepan. Cook until the mixture is melted. Beat the cream in a bowl until fluffy. Cut the cake into three layers. Place the bottom layer in a plate and top it with 2 tablespoon mint syrup, ½ cup whipped cream and 1 tablespoon crushed candies. Repeat these layers. Top the cake layers with the remaining whipped cream and the candies. Serve.

Gramma's Date Squares

Preparation time: 15 minutes
Cook time: 25 minutes
Nutrition facts (per serving): 119 Cal (9g fat, 4g protein, 0.5g fiber)

The famous date squares are here to make your Canadian cuisine extra special. Serve with some chocolate syrup on top.

Ingredients (8 servings)
1 ½ cups rolled oats
1 ½ cups sifted pastry flour
¼ teaspoon salt
¾ teaspoon baking soda
1 cup packed brown sugar
¾ cup butter, softened
¾ lb. pitted dates, diced
1 cup water
⅓ cup packed brown sugar
1 teaspoon lemon juice

Preparation
At 350 degrees F, preheat your oven. Mix the baking soda, 1 cup brown sugar, salt, pastry flour, and oats in a large bowl until crumbly. Spread half of this prepared mixture in a 9-inch baking pan. Mix ⅓ cup of brown sugar, water, and dates in a small saucepan and cook the mixture until it boils. Reduce its heat and cook until the mixture thickens. Add the lemon juice, mix, and remove from the heat. Spread this prepared mixture over the base and add the crumb mixture on top. Bake the layers for 25 minutes in the oven. Cut the layers into squares and serve.

Canadian Squares

Preparation time: 15 minutes
Cook time: 40 minutes
Nutrition facts (per serving): 411 Cal (9g fat, 11g protein, 7g fiber)

When you can't think of anything to serve as the dessert, then these delicious squares will help you big time to enjoy the authentic Canadian flavors.

Ingredients (6 servings)
Base
1 cup all-purpose flour
2 tablespoon confectioners' sugar
½ cup butter
⅓ cup seedless raspberry jam

Filling
⅔ cup white sugar
½ cup butter, softened
2 eggs
⅔ cup rice flour
10 drops red food coloring

Icing
2 cups confectioners' sugar
⅓ cup butter, softened
1 tablespoon milk
1 teaspoon maple extract

Preparation

At 300 degrees F, preheat your oven. Layer an 8-inch square baking pan with baking spray. Mix ½ cup of butter, 2 tablespoons of sugar, and 1 cup of flour in a bowl. Spread this prepared mixture in the prepared pan. Bake the crust for 20 minutes. Top this base with the raspberry jam. At 375 degrees F, preheat your oven. Beat sugar with ½ cup butter in a bowl until pale. Stir in the rice flour and mix evenly. Add the red color and then mix well. Spread this prepared mixture over the jam layer. Bake the batter for 20 minutes. Allow the pink squares to cool for 20 minutes. Beat 2 cups sugar, milk, maple, and ⅓ cup of butter in a bowl until fluffy. Spread this prepared mixture over the baked layers and allow it to cool. Cut into squares. Serve.

West Coast Trail Cookies

Preparation time: 10 minutes
Cook time: 12 minutes
Nutrition facts (per serving): 326 Cal (17g fat, 14g protein, 1.2g fiber)

Here's another classic recipe for your desserts collection. Serve these cookies with a delicious hot chocolate drink and enjoy the best of them.

Ingredients (6 servings)
1 cup all-purpose flour
½ cup whole wheat flour
⅓ cup flax seed meal
1 teaspoon ground cinnamon
½ teaspoon baking soda
¼ teaspoon salt
1 cup unsalted butter, softened
1 cup dark brown sugar
½ cup white sugar
2 eggs
2 teaspoon vanilla extract
2 cups rolled oats
1 cup semisweet chocolate chips
1 cup dried cranberries
¾ cup unsweetened shredded coconut
½ cup pumpkin seeds, chopped

Preparation

At 350 degrees F, preheat your oven. Layer 2 baking sheets with parchment paper. Mix the flour with salt, baking soda, cinnamon, flaxseed meal, and whole wheat flour in a bowl. Beat the butter, 1 cup brown sugar, and white sugar in a bowl until creamy. Stir in the vanilla and the eggs and then beat well. Stir in the flour mixture and mix until it makes smooth dough. Fold in the pumpkin seeds, coconut, cranberries, oats, and chocolate chips and mix evenly. Make 1 ½ inch balls from this prepared dough and place them on a baking sheet. Flatten these balls and bake for 12 minutes. Allow the cookies to cool for 10 minutes. Serve.

Vancouver Island Cookies

Preparation time: 10 minutes
Cook time: 12 minutes
Nutrition facts (per serving): 567 Cal (26g fat, 29g protein, 1.2g fiber)

Try these super cookies to serve for all. Due to the use of oats, vanilla, spices, and sugars in the cookies, they have a great taste and good nutritional content.

Ingredients (4 servings)
1½ cups all-purpose flour
1 tablespoon baking powder
1 tablespoon baking soda
1½ tablespoon ground cinnamon
1 tablespoon ground nutmeg
1 tablespoon ground allspice
2 pinches salt
1 cup margarine, softened
1 cup white sugar
½ cup brown sugar
1 egg
3 tablespoon molasses
1 tablespoon vanilla extract
1½ cups quick cooking oats
1 cup sweetened flaked coconut

Preparation

At 350 degrees F, preheat your oven. Grease 2 baking sheets with cooking spray. Mix the flour, salt, allspice, nutmeg, cinnamon, baking soda, baking powder, and flour in a bowl. Beat the margarine with brown sugar and white sugar with an electric mixture in a bowl until smooth. Stir in the vanilla, molasses, and egg and then blend well. Add the flour mixture and then mix until smooth. Fold in the coconut and the oats and then mix well. Make 1 ¼ inch balls from this prepared mixture. Place the balls in the baking sheets, bake for 12 minutes, and then allow the balls to cool. Serve.

Classic Butter Tarts

Preparation time: 15 minutes
Cook time: 10 minutes
Nutrition facts (per serving): 347 Cal (5g fat, 7g protein, 5g fiber)

A dessert that has no parallel, the Canadian butter tarts are made with flour and corn syrup filling. As a result, the combination tastes heavenly.

Ingredients (6 servings)

1 ¾ cups whole-wheat flour
1 egg yolk
⅓ cup butter, cubed
¼ cup lard, diced
1 teaspoon white vinegar
½ teaspoon salt
¼ cup ice water

Filling

2 tablespoon maple syrup
¾ cup brown sugar
⅓ cup white corn syrup
2 eggs
¼ cup unsalted butter, melted
1 teaspoon vanilla
1 teaspoon white vinegar
⅛ teaspoon salt

Preparation

Mix the flour with salt, lard, and butter in a food processor until crumbly. Add the ice water, vinegar, and yolk; then mix until the mixture is smooth. Cover and refrigerate the prepared dough for 1 hour. At 450 degrees F, preheat your oven at 450 degrees F. Mix the sugar, salt, vinegar, vanilla, butter, eggs, corn sugar, and maple syrup in a bowl until smooth. Roll out the prepared dough into ⅛-inch-thick sheet. Cut the prepared dough into 12 rounds using 4 ½ inch cookie cutters. Place each cookie round in each muffin cup and press it. Cover and refrigerate the prepared dough rounds for 20 minutes. Bake the cookie rounds for 8 minutes. Reduce its heat to 400 degrees F then add filling to the crust. Bake the tart for 7 minutes. Allow the cooked tarts to cool for 3 minutes. Serve.

Duchess Doughnut

Preparation time: 15 minutes
Cook time: 8 minutes
Nutrition facts (per serving): 221 Cal (3 g fat, 4 g protein, 2.8g fiber)

Yes, you can make something as delicious as these Canadian doughnuts by using only basic dessert ingredients and some simple techniques.

Ingredients (6 servings)
1 cup sultana raisins
1 cup 2% milk
1 teaspoon instant yeast
¼ cup granulated sugar
¼ cup unsalted butter, melted
1 egg
½ teaspoon salt
2 ½ cups all-purpose flour
Canola oil, for frying

Glaze
2 cups icing sugar
¼ cup water

Preparation
Soak the raisins in 1 cup boiling water in a bowl for 10 minutes and then drain. Warm the milk in a bowl for 45 seconds. Add the yeast, mix well, and leave for 10 minutes. Stir in the flour, salt, egg, butter, sugar, and raisins; then mix well until it makes a smooth dough for 5 minutes.

Transfer this prepared dough to a greased bowl, cover, and leave the prepared dough for 1 hour. Layer a baking sheet with parchment paper. Roll the prepared dough into ½ inch thick square and cut into 12 squares. Place each square in the baking sheet, cover, and leave for 45 minutes. Set a deep pan with oil and heat to 400 degrees F. Deep fry the prepared dough for 4 minutes per side. Transfer the cooked donuts to a plate, lined with paper towel. Mix the icing sugar with water in a bowl and pour over the donuts. Serve.

Apple Dutch Baby

Preparation time: 10 minutes
Cook time: 15 minutes
Nutrition facts (per serving): 223 Cal (10g fat, 6g protein, 0.8g fiber)

This Apple Dutch baby will leave you spellbound due to the mildly sweet taste and the combination of sugar toppings.

Ingredients (6 servings)
¼ cup butter, diced
3 tart apples, peeled and sliced
¼ cup packed brown sugar
1 teaspoon ground cinnamon
6 large eggs, separated
⅔ cup all-purpose flour
⅓ cup 2% milk
1 teaspoon baking powder
½ teaspoon salt
¼ cup sugar
Confectioners' sugar, optional

Preparation
At 400 degrees F, preheat your oven. Grease a 13x9 inch baking dish with butter. Mix the apples, cinnamon, and brown sugar in a bowl, spread the apples in the baking dish, and then bake for 18 minutes. Beat the egg yolks with salt, baking powder, milk and flour in a small bowl until smooth. Beat the egg whites in a bowl until they form peaks. Add the sugar and beat until the mixture is foamy. Add the fluffed egg whites to the yolk mixture, mix well, and spread over the apples. Bake the apples for 15 minutes. Garnish with sugar and serve.

PB&J Bites

Preparation time: 30 minutes
Nutrition facts (per serving): 185 Cal (12g fat, 6g protein, 0.4g fiber)

If you want something exotic on your dessert menu, then nothing can taste better than these delicious homemade PB&J bites.

Ingredients (6 servings)
1 ½ cups quick-cooking oats
1 cup creamy peanut butter
½ cup confectioners' sugar
6 teaspoon favorite jam

Preparation
Blend 1 cup oats with sugar and peanut butter in a food processor. Make 1 ¼ inch balls from this prepared mixture and flatten them into cookies. Place the cookies in a baking sheet and press the center of each cookie. Add ½ teaspoon jam at the center of each cookie. Refrigerate for 30 minutes and serve.

Butterscotch Fudge

Preparation time: 15 minutes
Cook time: 10 minutes
Nutrition facts (per serving): 201 Cal (6g fat, 4g protein, 0.6g fiber)

The Canadian butterscotch fudge has no parallel. It's quick and simple make at home if you have marshmallows and butter.

Ingredients (8 servings)

1 teaspoon 2 tablespoon butter
1 ⅔ cups sugar
⅔ cup evaporated milk
½ teaspoon salt
2 cups miniature marshmallows
1 package (11 oz.) butterscotch chips
½ cup chopped walnuts, toasted
1 teaspoon maple flavoring

Preparation

Layer an 8-inch square pan with a foil sheet and grease with 1 teaspoon butter. Mix the remaining 2 tablespoon butter, salt, milk, and sugar in a large saucepan, cook the mixture to a boil, and mix well. Remove this prepared mixture from the heat and stir in the marshmallows, nuts, maple flavoring, and butterscotch chips. Cook until the mixture is melted. Spread this prepared mixture in the square pan and allow it to cool. Cut the fudge into 1-inch squares. Serve.

Cherry Nanaimo Bars

Preparation time: 15 minutes
Cook time: 8 minutes
Nutrition facts (per serving): 118 Cal (17g fat, 1g protein, 8g fiber)

Nanaimo bars are the specialty of the Canadian dessert menu. Now you can try them in cherry flavor using this simple recipe.

Ingredients (6 servings)
Bottom Layer
½ cup butter
¼ cup white sugar
⅓ cup unsweetened cocoa powder
1 egg, lightly beaten
1 ¾ cups graham cracker crumbs
½ cup shredded coconut
⅓ cup chopped walnuts

Middle Layer
¼ cup butter, softened
2 cups confectioners' sugar
2 tablespoon maraschino cherry juice
1 teaspoon almond extract
⅓ cup chopped maraschino cherries, well drained

Top Layer
1 tablespoon butter
⅓ cup semisweet chocolate chips

Preparation

Mix the sugar, cocoa powder and ½ cup butter in a saucepan and cook over medium heat for 2 minutes. Remove this prepared mixture from the heat and stir in beaten egg. Stir and cook this prepared mixture for 3 minutes. Remove this prepared mixture from the heat. Add the walnuts, coconut and crumbs then mix well. Spread this prepared mixture in a 9x9 inch baking pan. Beat ¼ cup butter with almond extract, cherry juice, and sugar in a beater until smooth. Stir in cherries and mix evenly. Spread this prepared mixture over the crumb crust. Melt 1 tablespoon butter and chocolate chips in a pan for 3 minutes. Pour this chocolate over the layer then refrigerate for 30 minutes. Cut into bars and serve.

Maple Meringues

Preparation time: 15 minutes
Cook time: 60 minutes
Nutrition facts (per serving): 286 Cal (11g fat, 2g protein, 3g fiber)

These maple meringues are a must-have as a snack or a dessert. In turn, with the help of this recipe, you can cook them in no time.

Ingredients (8 servings)
4 egg whites
¼ teaspoon cream of tartar
¾ cup granulated sugar
¼ cup confectioners' sugar
½ teaspoon maple flavored extract

Preparation
At 300 degrees F, preheat your oven. Layer the cookie sheets with baking paper. Beat the 4 egg whites and the cream of tartar in a bowl until foamy. Stir in the sugar and beat until foamy. Add maple syrup, mix well, and transfer this prepared mixture to a piping bag. Pipe the mixture on the cookie sheets into 1-inch circles. Reduce the oven's heat to 250 degrees F and bake the meringue for 60 minutes. Allow the meringues to cool and serve.

Nanaimo Bars

Preparation time: 10 minutes
Cook time: 5 minutes
Nutrition facts (per serving): 227 Cal (15g fat, 11g protein, 2.1g fiber)

The Nanaimo bars are the best dessert to find in the Canadian cuisine. They're loaded with nutrients as prepared with butter, chocolate, coconut, and crumbs.

Ingredients (8 servings)

Bottom Layer
½ cup unsalted butter, diced
¼ cup granulated sugar
5 tablespoon unsweetened cocoa powder
⅛ teaspoon salt
1 large egg, beaten
1 ¾ cup graham cracker crumbs
½ cup almonds, chopped
1 cup sweetened shredded coconut

Filling
½ cup unsalted butter, softened
2 - 3 Tablespoon heavy cream
2 Tablespoon Bird's custard powder
1 ¾ cups powdered sugar

Top Layer
4 oz semi-sweet chocolate, chopped
2 tablespoon unsalted butter

Preparation
Grease an 8x8inch baking dish with butter and spread a baking paper. Mix the melted butter with the salt, cocoa powder, and sugar in a saucepan. Stir in the beaten egg, mix well, and cook until the mixture thickens. Remove this prepared mixture from the heat and stir in the almonds, coconut, and crumbs. Mix well and spread this prepared mixture in the prepared baking pan and allow it cool. Meanwhile, mix 2 tablespoon of heavy cream, custard powder, butter, and sugar in a bowl. Spread this prepared mixture in the prepared layer. Refrigerate these layers for 30 minutes. Melt the butter and the chocolate in a bowl by heating in the microwave for 20 seconds. Spread this melted chocolate over the refrigerated layers and refrigerate again for 1 hour. Cut the layers into squares. Serve.

Rhubarb Crumble Ice Cream

Preparation time: 15 minutes
Cook time: 11 minutes
Nutrition facts (per serving): 228 Cal (6g fat, 4g protein, 3g fiber)

Canadian rhubarb ice cream is one good option for desserts. You can also keep them ready and stored, then use them instead as instant treats.

Ingredients (8 servings)
3 cups fresh rhubarb, diced
⅔ cup ¾ cup sugar
⅔ cup water
1 tablespoon butter
⅓ cup quick-cooking oats
1 tablespoon brown sugar
¼ teaspoon ground cinnamon
1-½ cups heavy whipping cream
1-½ cups half-and-half cream
1 teaspoon vanilla extract

Preparation
Mix ⅔ cup sugar, water and rhubarb in a small saucepan and cook the mixture to a bowl. Reduce the heat and cook the mixture on a simmer for 10 minutes. Allow the mixture to cool. Sauté the oats with cinnamon, and brown sugar in a skillet for 1 minute. Beat the creams with sugar and vanilla in a bowl. Transfer this prepared mixture to an ice cream maker and churn as per the machine's instructions. Stir in the oat mixture and mix evenly. Spread ½ of the ice cream in a 1-quart freezer container and top it with the rhubarb mixture. Repeat the layers, cover, and freeze for 4 hours. Slice and serve.

Chocolate-Covered Cheesecake Squares

Preparation time: 10 minutes
Cook time: 40 minutes
Nutrition facts (per serving): 141 Cal (10g fat, 2g protein, 1.1g fiber)

Here comes a dessert that's beloved by all. The cheesecake squares are not only served as a dessert, but they're also a famous snack in Canada.

Ingredients (6 servings)
1 cup graham cracker crumbs
¼ cup chopped pecans
¼ cup butter, melted

Filling
2 packages (8 oz.) cream cheese, softened
½ cup sugar
¼ cup sour cream
2 large eggs, beaten
½ teaspoon vanilla extract

Coating
24 oz. semisweet chocolate, chopped
3 tablespoon shortening

Preparation
Mix the graham cracker crumbs with butter and pecans in a small bowl. Layer a 9-inch baking pan with a foil sheet. Spread the crumb mixture in a baking pan. Beat the filling ingredients in a bowl and spread in the

crust. Bake the layers for 40 minutes at 325 degrees F. Allow the layers to cool. Mix the chocolate and the shortening in a bowl and melt in the microwave. Pour the melted chocolate on top. Allow the layers to cool and cut into squares. Serve.

Drinks

Canadian Cocktail

Preparation time: 10 minutes
Nutrition facts (per serving): 218 Cal (8g fat, 4g protein, 1g fiber)

This Canadian cocktail famous for its blend of whiskey, orange liqueur, and lemon juice. You can prep this drink easily at home.

Ingredients (2 servings)
1 ½ oz. Canadian whisky
½ oz. orange liqueur
½ oz. lemon juice
1 teaspoon simple syrup
1 dash bitters

Preparation
Mix all the Canadian cocktail ingredients in a cocktail shaker. Serve.

Classic Caesar

Preparation time: 5 minutes
Nutrition facts (per serving): 203 Cal (11g fat, 1g protein, 0g fiber)

The Canadian Caesar drink is all that you need to celebrate the winter holidays. Keep the drink ready in your refrigerator for quick serving.

Ingredients (2 serving)
3 dashes of Worcestershire sauce
3 oz. clamato juice
1-3 dashes hot sauce
1-2 oz. vodka
1 pinch salt
1 pinch black pepper
Olives, pickles, for garnishes

Preparation
Mix all the Caesar cocktail ingredients in a cocktail shaker. Serve.

Canadian Maple Old-Fashioned

Preparation time: 5 minutes
Nutrition facts (per serving): 286 Cal (7g fat, 4g protein, 1g fiber)

Here's a special Canadian old-fashioned drink made from whiskey, maple, and angostura bitters. Serve fresh for best taste.

Ingredients (2 servings)
½ cup ice
2 oz. Canadian whiskey
2 teaspoon maple syrup
2 dashes Angostura bitters
1-2 maraschino cherries
1 slice orange peel expressed

Preparation
Mix all the old-fashioned cocktail ingredients in a cocktail shaker. Serve.

Canadian Punch

Preparation time: 5 minutes
Nutrition facts (per serving): 207 Cal (1g fat, 1g protein, 1.3g fiber)

Made with rye whiskey, pineapple, and lemon juice, this beverage is a refreshing addition to the Canadian cocktail menu.

Ingredients (6 servings)
16 oz. rye whiskey
8 oz. traditional Jamaica rum
3 lemons, sliced
1 pineapple, peeled, cored and sliced
¾ cup sugar
5 cups water
1 quart-sized ice block
Grated nutmeg

Preparation
Mix all the Canadian punch ingredients in a cocktail shaker. Serve.

Canadian Whiskey Sour

Preparation time: 10 minutes
Nutrition facts (per serving): 106 Cal (0g fat, 0g protein, 9g fiber)

This refreshing whiskey cocktail is always a delight to serve at parties. Now you can make it easily at home by using the following simple ingredients.

Ingredients (2 servings)

1 oz. Canadian rye whiskey
1 oz. pure Canadian maple syrup
1 oz. fresh lemon juice
Ice

Preparation

Mix all the whiskey sour ingredients in a cocktail shaker. Serve.

If you liked Canadian recipes, discover to how cook DELICIOUS recipes from neighboring **Balkan** countries!

Within these pages, you'll learn 35 authentic recipes from a Balkan cook. These aren't ordinary recipes you'd find on the Internet, but recipes that were closely guarded by our Balkan mothers and passed down from generation to generation.

Main Dishes, Appetizers, and Desserts included!

If you want to learn how to make Croatian green peas stew, and 32 other authentic Balkan recipes, then start with our book!

Order at www.balkanfood.org/cook-books/ for only $2,99!

Maybe Hungarian cuisine?

Order at www.balkanfood.org/cook-books/ for only $2,99!

If you're a **Mediterranean** dieter who wants to know the secrets of the Mediterranean diet, dieting, and cooking, then you're about to discover how to master cooking meals on a Mediterranean diet right now!

In fact, if you want to know how to make Mediterranean food, then this new e-book - "The 30-minute Mediterranean diet" - gives you the answers to many important questions and challenges every Mediterranean dieter faces, including:

- How can I succeed with a Mediterranean diet?
- What kind of recipes can I make?
- What are the key principles to this type of diet?
- What are the suggested weekly menus for this diet?
- Are there any cheat items I can make?

... and more!

If you're serious about cooking meals on a Mediterranean diet and you really want to know how to make Mediterranean food, then you need to grab a copy of "The 30-minute Mediterranean diet" right now.

Prepare **111 recipes with several ingredients in less than 30 minutes**!

Order at www.balkanfood.org/cook-books/ for only $2,99!

What could be better than a home-cooked meal? Maybe only a **Greek** homemade meal.

Do not get discouraged if you have no Greek roots or friends. Now you can make a Greek food feast in your kitchen.

This ultimate Greek cookbook offers you 111 best dishes of this cuisine! From more famous gyros to more exotic *Kota Kapama* this cookbook keeps it easy and affordable.

All the ingredients necessary are wholesome and widely accessible. The author's picks are as flavorful as they are healthy. The dishes described in this cookbook are "what Greek mothers have made for decades."

Full of well-balanced and nutritious meals, this handy cookbook includes many vegan options. Discover a plethora of benefits of Mediterranean cuisine, and you may fall in love with cooking at home.

Inspired by a real food lover, this collection of delicious recipes will taste buds utterly satisfied.

Order at www.balkanfood.org/cook-books/ for only $2,99!

Maybe some Swedish meatballs?

Order at www.balkanfood.org/cook-books/ for only $2,99!

Maybe to try exotic **Syrian** cuisine?

From succulent *sarma*, soups, warm and cold salads to delectable desserts, the plethora of flavors will satisfy the most jaded foodie. Have a taste of a new culture with this **traditional Syrian cookbook**.

Order at www.balkanfood.org/cook-books/ for only $2,99!

Maybe **Polish** cuisine?

Order at www.balkanfood.org/cook-books/ for only $2,99!

Or **Peruvian?**

Order at www.balkanfood.org/cook-books/ for only $2,99!

ONE LAST THING

If you enjoyed this book or found it useful, I'd be very grateful if you could find the time to post a short review on Amazon. Your support really does make a difference and I read all the reviews personally, so I can get your feedback and make this book even better.

Thanks again for your support!

Please send me your feedback at

www.balkanfood.org

Printed in Great Britain
by Amazon